The Choctaws

BIBLIOGRAPHICAL SERIES
*The Newberry Library Center
for the History of the American Indian*

General Editor
Francis Jennings

Assistant Editor
William R. Swagerty

The Center is Supported by Grants from

The National Endowment for the Humanities
The Ford Foundation
The W. Clement and Jessie V. Stone Foundation
The Woods Charitable Fund, Inc.
Mr. Gaylord Donnelley
The Andrew W. Mellon Foundation
The Robert R. McCormick Charitable Trust
The John D. and Catherine T. McArthur Foundation

The Choctaws

A Critical Bibliography

CLARA SUE KIDWELL

AND

CHARLES ROBERTS

Published for the Newberry Library

Indiana University Press

BLOOMINGTON

Manufactured in the United States of America

Library of Congress Cataloging in Publication Data

Kidwell, Clara Sue.
  The Choctaws.

  (Bibliographical series)
  Includes index.
  1.Choctaw Indians—History—Bibliography.
I.Roberts, Charles, 1941– joint author. II.Title.
Z1210.C53K52 [E99.C8] 016.970004'97 80–8037
ISBN 0–253–34412–3 (pbk.) 1 2 3 4 5 84 83 82 81 80

CONTENTS

INTRODUCTION

The Muskhogean-speaking Choctaws were at one time a large group of native Americans residing in the Southeastern United States. They are known as one of the Five Civilized Tribes because they so quickly adopted much of the culture of the Europeans who came into their neighborhood. Yet they have maintained a distinctive tribal identity to the present day. In the earliest written records, they appear as a numerous, settled horticultural people living in the lower Mississippi valley. They were among the first native peoples of North America to experience European invasion, lying along the campaign path of Hernando de Soto in the winter of 1540–41, and they resisted the conquistadores fiercely. From that time forward, Choctaw history has been intertwined with the lives of Europeans and Euramericans as well as Afro-Americans and other Indians.

During the era of European colonial expansion, the Choctaws were spread across the frontier of interaction between Spanish Florida, French Louisiana, and the English Carolinas, and they were heavily involved in the intrigues of the colonial powers and their Indian allies. They were an important presence on the American side during the American Revolution. Though they adopted the forms of European civilization and were influenced more than any of the other Five Civilized Tribes by Christian missionaries, the majority of the tribe were forced in the 1830s to travel "the trail of tears" to Indian Territory beyond the Mississippi River. Those who remained behind in the state of Mississippi after the 1830s became a landless Indian minority in a society where people were defined as either White or colored. Those who moved to Oklahoma established a flourishing nation that was once again subjected to the land hunger of American expansionists. As civilized slave owners, the Choctaws were embroiled tragically in the Civil War. The westward march of the transcontinental railroad and the pressure for opening up "the public domain" in the late nineteenth and early twentieth centuries overwhelmed the Choctaw Nation in Indian Territory as it had overwhelmed the tribe in Mississippi.

In 1907, with the admission of Oklahoma as a state of the Union, the Choctaw Nation ceased to exist as a sovereign entity. The dissolution of the Choctaw government did not, however, lead to the disappearance of the Choctaws in Oklahoma, any more than it had led to their disappearance as a distinctive group in Mississippi. The legal status of these peoples has undergone significant changes, and missionary and educational activities have certainly led to adaptation and change for the Choctaws both in Mississippi and in Oklahoma. However, in both states there are still distinctive communities and a strong sense of identification with the historical traditions of the tribe and with their contemporary situation. A good deal has been written about the Choctaws in Oklahoma, but very little attention has been paid to those in Mississippi and Louisiana.

The Choctaws have been subject to the major pressures that history has put upon Indian people to assimilate and to acculturate to American culture. The division of the tribe between Mississippi and Oklahoma is a result of differing responses to those pressures. And yet the continuity of identity between the historic communities that were first encountered by Hernando de Soto in 1540 and the Choctaws of the present day cannot be overlooked. For this reason, the history of the Choctaws represents a fascinating study of a group of people who have been involved in the major events of American history but who have also remained distinctively apart from the mainstream of American society.

RECOMMENDED WORKS

For the Beginner

[13]   W. David Baird, *The Choctaw People.*

[70]   Arthur H. DeRosier, Jr., *The Removal of the Choctaw Indians.*

[135]   R. A. Lafferty, *Okla Hannali.*

[208]   John R. Swanton, *Source Material for the Social and Ceremonial Life of the Choctaw Indians.*

[231]   Muriel H. Wright, *A Guide to the Indian Tribes of Oklahoma.*

For a Basic Library

[1]   Annie Heloise Abel, *The American Indian as Slaveholder and Secessionist.*

[9]   M. Thomas Bailey, *Reconstruction in Indian Territory.*

[12]   W. David Baird, *Peter Pitchlynn, Chief of the Choctaws.*

[17]   Henry C. Benson, *Life among the Choctaw Indians and Sketches of the South-West.*

[178] James H. O'Donnell, III, *Southern Indians in the American Revolution.*

[209] John R. Swanton, *The Indians of the Southeastern United States.*

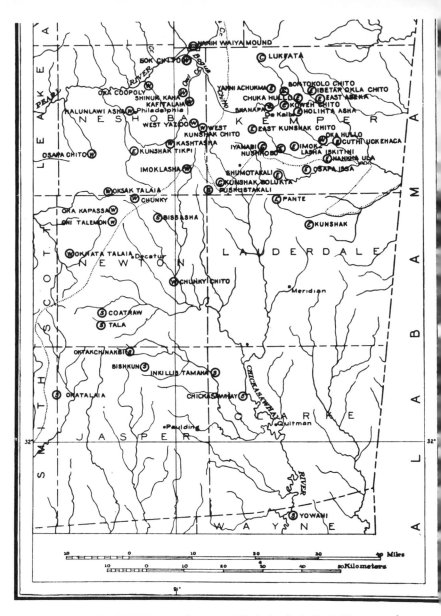

Map 1. The Old Choctaw Country, Mississippi. *C, E, S, W*—towns belonging to the central, eastern, southern, and western divisions of the nation. The dotted lines indicate the boundaries between the three latter divisions in the early part of the nineteenth century. From John R. Swanton, *Source Material for the Social and Ceremonial Life of the Choctaw Indians* [208, plate 3].

BIBLIOGRAPHICAL ESSAY

Archaeology and Ethnography

The Choctaws shared with most other southeastern Indians strong cultural influences from the Mississippian tradition. Traveling through the Southeast in 1540, Hernando de Soto encountered very populous societies with powerful chiefs and large ceremonial centers. The town of Mavilla, where some 2,500 Indians were reportedly killed in a desperate battle of resistance against the Spanish army, probably served as the capital of a Mississippian "province" extending up the Tombigbee and Alabama river valleys. The huge prehistoric site at Moundville, situated just east of what later became known as Chata Yakni, or Choctaw country, vividly represents the Mississippian culture complex to modern visitors. Although the connection between Mississippian peoples of the sixteenth century and the Choctaws of the late seventeenth century remains unclear, the archaeological research at Moundville [152, 180, 220] and the narratives of the Hernando de Soto expedition, especially that of the Gentleman of Elvas [21, 190, 216], provide essential starting points for any study of Choctaw culture history.

Archaeological study of historic Choctaw sites is now under way by the Mississippi Department of Archives and History. Most published reports of artifacts to date are more antiquarian than archaeological. Henry B. Collins [49] has described in some detail potsherds found at village sites. The most recent report by John T. Penman in "Historic Choctaw Towns of the Southern Division" [181] attempts in a preliminary way to correlate archaeological data with historical descriptions of Choctaw villages. The reconstruction of a Choctaw village near Memphis, Tennessee, and its relationship to prehistoric sites are discussed by Charles H. Nash in *Chucalissa: Excavations and Burials through 1963* [176]. Richard A. Marshall, director of the Mississippi Archaeological Survey, provides a concise discussion of archaeological evidence within the state in "The Prehistory of Mississippi" [157].

The Choctaws themselves trace their origins as a nation to the sacred mound called Nanih Waiya, situated near the source of the Pearl River in present-day Winston County, Mississippi. According to one legend recorded by Gideon Lincecum in the early nineteenth century [142], the Choctaw people migrated southeastward from lands across the Mississippi River under a leader named Chata. Each morning they started moving in the direction pointed by a sacred pole that Chata had planted in the ground. Finally they awoke at their encampment by the Pearl River and discovered that for the first time the stick was standing straight up. On that spot these people deposited the bones of their ancestors, which they had carried throughout the journey, and covered them with a large mound. Another version obtained by Henry Halbert from Isaac Pistonatubbee toward the end of the nineteenth century tells how the Choctaws and neighboring tribes ascended from a hole in the earth not far from Nanih Waiya [104]. For a description of this mound and how it has changed in size and appearance, see Halbert's "Nanih Waiya, the Sacred Mound of the Choctaws" [108].

In *Source Material for the Social and Ceremonial Life of the Choctaw Indians* [208], John R. Swanton compiled both his own fieldwork and most of the historical information available to him to produce what is still the most comprehensive study of the Choctaw people. Writing in a world on the brink of unprecedented war, Swanton emphasized what he called the Choctaws' "enviable position of being 'just folks.'" His argument that they grew as a nation by economic rather than political and military means and that they "became with great rapidity poor subjects for ethnological study but successful members of the American Nation" had a strong influence upon subsequent students. Consequently we know much more about the material side of Choctaw culture than about any other aspect.

Swanton's *Source Material* nonetheless provides the best springboard for further inquiry into Choctaw history. The extensive list of towns with their approximate locations and the sources of information regarding each, for example, is an extremely useful tool for historians who may want to identify and map Choctaw villages as they were during the eighteenth century. Swanton also derived from various sources a sketch of the political organization of the Choctaws that existed throughout the colonial period of their history. Although the individual town was the political and economic focus of Choctaw life, villages were divided into at least three separate groups. Towns in the western part of the nation belonged to Okla Falaya, or the Long People; those in the east were called Okla Tannap, People of the Opposite Side; and in the southern area lived the Okla Hannali, or the Sixtowns People. Each division had its own chief in addition to the national chief, but these positions were not confined to particular villages.

Choctaw social organization, like that of other Mississippian cultures, was extremely complex and multilevel. Two groups of people, usually described as "upper" and "lower," existed at the tribal or aggregate level. These groups were separated into moieties, Ihulahta and Imoklasha, which operated by an exogamous marriage relationship and by matrilineal descent. Each moiety consisted of three clans. This dual division of Choctaw society functioned as a fundamental mechanism of social cohesion by not only requiring intermarriage across villages but also meeting governmental and ceremonial needs. Persons accused of criminal behavior were tried before their own moieties. The moieties also performed complementary services for each other during the Choctaws' elaborate funeral rites.

Probably the most distinguishing feature of Choctaw culture was the practice of allowing the bodies of their dead to decompose on raised platforms and having a class of "bone-pickers" scrape away the remaining flesh with their fingernails. The bones were then carefully stored and periodically brought out for mourning ceremonies. Another practice that seemed to distinguish the Choctaws from other southeastern tribes was flattening the foreheads of their infants with weights as they lay in cradleboards. Both burial customs and head deformation drew the attention of many early White observers, who criticized the Choctaws for these "uncivil" practices. James Adair, in "An Account of the Chocktah Nations," a chapter of his 1775 *History of the American Indians,* typifies this colonial English attitude in this statement [4, p. 284]: "The Chocktah flatten their foreheads with a bag of sand, which with great care they keep fastened on the scull of the infant, while it is in its tender and imperfect state. Thus they quite deform their face, and give themselves an appearance, which is disagreeable to any but those of their own likeness."

The eighteenth-century literature on the Choctaws is replete with critical statements like that of Adair. By the nineteenth century, however, it appears that pressures by the dominant Euramerican society to suppress the traditional burial activities of the bone-pickers as well as head deformation of infants were successful in bringing about the gradual abandonment of these traditional practices.

Important social activities noted by early observers and still practiced by Choctaws today include the annual Green Corn Dance and the sport known as *ishtaboli,* or stickball. At each harvest festival the nation rekindled its sacred fire with song and dance. Throughout the year villages challenged each other to stickball, a game resembling lacrosse, played on a large field with much vigor and occasional violence. While the participants, up to a hundred on a side and each equipped with two cupped sticks, tossed a ball made of deerskin toward their respective goals, spectators gambled many of their possessions on their teams. The Choctaw Fair now held each summer by the Mississippi band highlights both the traditional harvest festival and the stickball championship played among Choctaw high-school teams. One eighteenth-century observer described the stickball game as follows [19, pp. 169–70]:

> An old man, standing in the middle of the field, throws up a deerskin ball. The players then run to try to catch the ball in their rackets. It is fun to watch them play naked, painted with all kinds of colors, and with a wildcat's tail tied behind them. The feathers attached to their arms and heads look odd as they wave back and forth in the wind. The players push and throw each other down. Anyone who is skillful enough to get the ball passes it on to a teammate, and his opponents try to get it away from him. Both teams play with such ardor that shoulders are often dislocated in the fray. The players never become angry, and the old men, who act as referees, remind them that they are playing for sport and not for blood. There is a great deal of gambling; even the women bet among themselves.
>
> When the men's game is finished, the women get together to play to avenge their husbands' losses. Their rackets are different from those that the men use in that they are bent. The women, who are very good at this game, run swiftly and push each other around just as the men do. They are dressed exactly like the men, but with a little more modesty. They put

red paint on their cheeks only and apply vermilion instead of powder to their hair.

After having played hard all day long, everyone goes home in glory or in shame. There is no bitterness as each one promises to play another day when the best man will win.

W. David Baird, *The Choctaw People* [13], and Jesse O. McKee and Jon A. Schlenker, *The Choctaws: Cultural Evolution of a Native American Tribe* [151], nicely summarize the major features of Choctaw culture and history. T. N. Campbell skillfully uses the notes and manuscripts left by Gideon Lincecum to discuss more specific aspects of life in "Choctaw Subsistence: Ethnographic Notes from the Lincecum Manuscript" [33], "The Choctaw Afterworld" [32], and "Medicinal Plants Used by Choctaw, Chickasaw and Creek Indians in the Early Nineteenth Century" [31]. Anyone particularly interested in Choctaw uses of plants, which were commented on frequently by early travelers, should see Lyda A. Taylor, *Plants Used as Curatives by Certain Southeastern Tribes* [211]. C. C. Copeland's "A Choctaw Tradition" [50] discusses traditional conceptions of the rising and setting of the sun.

More ethnographic information can be found in other publications by Swanton, especially *Indian Tribes of the Lower Mississippi Valley and Adjacent Coast of the Gulf of Mexico* [205], *Myths and Tales of the Southeastern Indians* [207], and *The Indians of the Southeastern United States* [209]. Important additions to the general literature on southeastern Indians include Jesse Burt and Robert B. Ferguson, *Indians of the Southeast: Then and*

Now [26], and Charles Hudson, *The Southeastern Indians* [126]. Hudson's excellent synthesis contributes greatly to our understanding of the spiritual as well as the material life of Indian tribes throughout this region.

Choctaw Relations with European Colonies

The establishment of relations between the Choctaw Indians and the French colony of Louisiana at the beginning of the eighteenth century followed a great number of disruptive years. During the seventeenth century, smallpox and other European diseases had probably entered their villages from the Spanish missions along the Florida coast. After the English founded their colony of Carolina in 1670, traders penetrated the southeastern interior in search of Indian slaves and deerskins. The Choctaws fell under repeated attack by Chickasaw and Creek raiders who were armed by the English and employed to capture slaves. By 1702, when they met with the French at Mobile for the first time, the Choctaws had lost some two thousand people by death, and another five hundred had been captured by English-led war parties. The French took advantage of these conditions and established a firm alliance with the Choctaw nation, which still numbered about four thousand warriors.

The alliance that resulted solidified Choctaw-French relations on the battlefield as well as in a growing trading nexus. With Spain, France, and the Choctaws in cooperation, the escalating confrontation known in America as Queen Anne's War led to increased factionalism among southeastern Indian groups as well as intensified European rivalry for control of the North American continent. While the Choctaws supported the French in their effort to gain a stronger foothold in America, the Creeks and Chickasaws sided with the British. These alliances served to rekindle several series of wars between the Choctaws and the Chickasaws in the first quarter of the eighteenth century and aided Europeans in augmenting their own forces while simultaneously eroding native manpower. Arrell M. Gibson's *The Chickasaws* [92] is particularly useful as an interpretation of Chickasaw-Choctaw relations during the eighteenth century. Verner W. Crane's *The Southern Frontier, 1670–1732* [53] is still the best secondary account of these important events in Choctaw history.

During the eighteenth century the colony of Louisiana developed strong trade and military connections with the Choctaws, who provided settlers with food as well as deerskins in exchange for European merchandise. Much of the correspondence among French officials includes information about the Choctaws and their participation in colonial trade and diplomacy. Dunbar Rowland and A. G. Sanders translated many of these documents and published three volumes of the *Mississippi Provincial Archives: French Dominion* [195]. The larger collection of official manuscripts from which these are taken is in the Mississippi Department of Archives and History at Jackson. Other published sources of official French material concerning the Choctaws include M. de Villiers du Terrage's "Documents concernant l'histoire des Indians de la région orientale de la Louisiane" [217] and "Notes sur les Chactas" [218].

In addition to exacerbating conflict with the Chickasaws, intercolonial rivalry between Great Britain and France posed many difficulties for the Choctaw people. British offers of trade on better terms and frequent shortages of goods among the French made it difficult for them to maintain a steadfast loyalty to Louisiana. During the Natchez War of 1729–31, which eventually drew the Choctaws—in alliance with the French—into a bitter war against the Natchez, it was rumored that the Choctaws had almost joined the revolt against the French settlement. But, at the request of colonial officials in New Orleans, they marched instead against the Indian rebels. The proximity of the French colony to their villages made trade and military alliances with Louisiana more reliable than such relations with distant English colonies.

During the 1730s, refugees of the Natchez nation were granted asylum by the Chickasaws. Together, war parties of Chickasaws and Natchez began to attack French convoys on the Mississippi River. To counteract this resistance to the colony, Louisiana officials rekindled Choctaw hostility toward the Chickasaws by offering bounties for enemy scalps. In 1736 Governor Bienville led a large-scale military expedition against the Chickasaw villages. More than five hundred Choctaw warriors participated in this campaign, which ended when Bienville's army suffered a deadly ambush. In the winter of 1739–40, the French attempted another massive expedition that included an army of a thousand French soldiers and hundreds of Indian allies. This campaign involved little fighting, and it ended when the Chickasaws agreed to cease their hostilities and turn over Natchez refugees. The Choctaws, however, continued to intimidate the Chickasaw villages during the 1740s in the service of the French colony. John Brice Harris's *From Old Mobile to Fort Assumption: A Story of the French Attempts to Colonize Louisiana and Destroy the Chickasaw Indians* [117] is a detailed chronicle of the Chickasaw campaigns. The events during this period are also studied in depth by Patricia Dillon Woods in her recent dissertation, "The Relations between the French of Colonial Louisiana and the Choctaw, Chickasaw and Natchez Indians, 1699–1762" [225].

Despite continued support provided by the Choctaws for French strategies in Louisiana, a growing dependence upon ammunition, cloth, and alcohol created internal tensions that surfaced after the Chickasaw wars. In 1746 a group of villages in the western district revolted against the French and decided to open relations with English traders. Sparked by a sexual assault upon the wife of Red Shoes, a chief already leaning toward the English, this rebellion reflected a widespread discontent over French colonial policy in Louisiana. Encouraged by colonial officials, the larger pro-French faction turned against these dissidents.

After Red Shoes was assassinated in the summer of 1747, civil war broke out and lasted until 1750. Charles W. Paape's unpublished 1946 dissertation, "The Choctaw Revolt: A Chapter in the Intercolonial Rivalry in the Old Southwest" [179], remains the only extensive study of this costly event in Choctaw history.

The cession of New Orleans and the west side of the Mississippi River to Spain and the cession of the entire eastern region to Great Britain in 1763 seriously altered the Choctaws' position in southeastern politics. No longer able to bargain between two opposing colonies, they fell under the jurisdiction of only one colony, British West Florida. English traders, with larger quantities of rum and less attachment to the Choctaw people, replaced French traders in their villages. The effects of this change, especially the abuse of Indian women and the excessive sale of alcohol, were eloquently described by Choctaw leaders who complained repeatedly to English officials at Mobile. Many of their speeches and other related documents have been edited by Dunbar Rowland in *Mississippi Provincial Archives: English Dominion* [194], the only published volume of English correspondence from the state archives in Jackson. With the outbreak of the American Revolution, conditions once again began to change for the Choctaw people. Their participation in the war, minor compared with that of many other eastern nations, is discussed in James H. O'Donnell, *Southern Indians in the American Revolution* [178]. By the Treaty of Paris in 1783, Spain extended its sovereignty to

Florida, while the new nation called the United States of America claimed most of the east bank of the Mississippi. The Choctaws once again found themselves situated between two powers in colonial competition.

Several historical memoirs and travel accounts written during the eighteenth century provide invaluable information about the customs and changes observed among the Choctaws. The most detailed and specific description of Choctaw life appears in an anonymous French manuscript entitled "Relation de la Louisiane," in the Edward E. Ayer Collection of the Newberry Library, Chicago. Swanton, who dates it about the middle of the century, translated and published that part of the manuscript pertaining to the Choctaws in "An Early Account of the Choctaw Indians" [206]. As in the case of all Euramerican observations of native American societies, the historian must consciously penetrate the author's racial and cultural biases in order to extract objective images of the people actually being discussed. Among the village activities described by this author are trade with Frenchmen, various ways of cooking corn, marriage and child-rearing, healing and conjuring, playing ball, and raising horses.

Throughout the eighteenth century the Choctaws lived in approximately fifty villages, all concentrated in the hill country of central Mississippi (see map 1). Villages were situated on large plains broken up by innumerable winding bayous. Some villages covered areas as large as three miles long and a mile wide. The cabins in these towns were congregated into separate hamlets divided from each other by bayous and swamps. On the lowlands separating hamlets and villages, the Choctaws planted large fields of corn, pumpkins, and melons. Each household also had a small garden in which the women raised beans, tobacco, and even vegetables adopted from French colonists. Choctaw villagers acquired other food sources from the surrounding forests, especially deer, bear oil, nuts, and fruits. Needless to say, their diet consisted of a wide variety of dishes. The author of the "Relation" provides us with a rare glimpse inside a Choctaw village [206, pp. 57–58]:

> Their house is nothing else than a cabin made of pieces of wood of the size of the leg, buried in the earth, and fastened together with *lianas,* which are very flexible bands. These cabins are surrounded with mud walls without window; the door is only from three to four feet in height. They are covered with bark of the cypress or the pine. A hole is left at the top of each gable-end to let the smoke out, for they make their fires in the middle of the cabins, which are a gunshot distance from each other. The inside is surrounded with cane beds raised from three to four feet from the ground on account of the fleas which exist there in quantities, because of the dirt. When they are lying down the savages never get up to make water and let it run through the canes of their bed. When lying down they have a skin of a deer or bear under them and a skin of a bison or a blanket above. These beds serve them as table and chair. They have by way of furniture only an earthen pot in which to cook their food, some earthen pans for the same purpose, and some fanners or sieves and hampers to prepare their corn, which is their usual nourishment. They pound it in a wooden crusher (pile) or mortar, which they make out of the trunk of a tree, hollowed by means of

burning embers. The pestle belonging to it is sometimes ten feel long and as small around as the arm. The upper end is an unshaped mass which serves to weigh it down and to give force to this pestle in falling back, in order to crush the corn more easily. After it is thus crushed they sift it in order to separate the finer part. They boil the coarser in a great skin which holds about three or four *sceau* of water, and mix it sometimes with pumpkins, or beans, or bean leaves. When this stew is almost cooked they throw into it the finest of the corn which they had reserved to thicken the water, and by way of seasoning they have a pot hung in the air in which are ashes of corn silk, beanpods, or finally oak ashes, on which having thrown water they take the lye which has fallen into a vessel provided underneath, and with it season their stew which is called *sagamite*.

Unlike the anonymous author of the "Relation," Antoine LePage du Pratz did not actually visit Choctaw villages. His great familiarity with the Natchez and deep interest in Indians, however, inspired him to devote much of his three-volume *Histoire de la Louisiane* [137] to native culture and history. Du Pratz's *Histoire,* which consistently refers to native Americans as "Indians" instead of using the conventional *sauvages,* is perhaps the most important single source for the study of Indian-French relations in the lower Mississippi Valley. Other more casual references to the Choctaws by travelers who skirted their villages can be found in Jean-Bernard Bossu, *Travels in the Interior of North America, 1751–1762* [19], and William Bartram, *Travels through North and South Carolina* [14].

After traveling through their villages during 1771–72, surveyor Bernard Romans wrote several interesting observations about the Choctaws in *A Concise Natural History of East and West Florida* [191]. Interspersed with this eighteenth-century English scientist's value judgments regarding hygiene, religion, and sexuality are useful details of life in villages and hunting camps, including a drawing of a Choctaw burial platform. Romans, a cartographer, also drew an important map naming and locating Choctaw towns, which was edited and annotated by Henry S. Halbert in "Bernard Romans' Map of 1772" [112]. In his *History*, Romans states that "the Choctaws may more properly be called a nation of farmers than any savages I have met with," observing that they produced surplus corn for both their Chickasaw neighbors and the colonists at Mobile. In an article entitled "The Nation of Bread" [223], William S. Willis challenges the accuracy of this statement, arguing that colonial conditions rather than any agrarian superiority over other southeastern tribes made the Choctaws dependent upon agricultural production.

As an English trader to the Chickasaws between 1744 and 1768, James Adair often visited Choctaw villages while attempting to divert their trade away from Louisiana. His *History of the American Indians* [4] includes a lengthy chapter on the Choctaws as well as many scattered comments concerning them. Notwithstanding his obsession with proving the Hebraic origins of native Americans, Adair demonstrates a very practical understanding of the Choctaws and their relations with European colonies.

Critical Years of Transition, 1783–1820

After the American Revolution, the Choctaws hoped to restore peaceful trade relations with colonists on the Gulf Coast who now lived under Spanish rule. Merchants in New Orleans, Mobile, and Pensacola— many of whom were Englishmen—traded aggressively with the Choctaws, Chickasaws, and Creeks for their deerskins. An important documentary source for Spanish relations with southern Indians during this period is Lawrence Kinnaird, editor, *Spain in the Mississippi Valley, 1765–1794* [132], three volumes of translated correspondence. Manuel Serrano y Sanz, *España y los Indios Cherokis y Chactas en la Segunda Mitad del Siglo XVIII* [199], and the present work of Jack D. L. Holmes provide important interpretations of Spain's Indian policy in the Southeast. Holmes's numerous articles include "Spanish Treaties with West Florida Indians, 1784–1802" [124], "Spanish Policy toward the Southern Indians in the 1790s" [125], and "The Choctaws in 1795" [123], the last being a detailed census found in the Louisiana Collection of the Bancroft Library of the University of California at Berkeley.

The Treaty of Hopewell in 1786 marked the official beginning of Choctaw relations with the United States. Although it stipulated that Congress "shall have the sole and exclusive right of regulating the trade with the Indians," the Choctaws continued to trade primarily with merchants in the Spanish provinces. By the 1790s, pressures of White settlement and scarcities of game caused Choctaw hunters to travel more frequently across the Mississippi River and eventually led to the permanent migration of many families toward the Red River. More dependent than ever upon European merchandise, the Choctaws fell into greater debt to merchants. Recognizing such trade debts as a means to obtain Indian lands, the United States government established its own trading posts among several nations, including one on the Tombigbee River in 1802. The 13 volumes relating to Indian Affairs in *The New American State Papers* [177] contain important information about these so-called trade factories as well as about treaties made with Indian nations. The Choctaw trade with the United States is discussed in Aloysius Plaisance, "The Choctaw Trading House, 1803–1822" [186].

Finding themselves within the jurisdiction of the Mississippi Territory after 1798, the Choctaws became more deeply involved in United States trade and diplomacy. Treaties ceding large sections of land began at the turn of the nineteenth century. In 1801 the Choctaws signed the Treaty of Fort Adams, ceding 2,641,920 acres of valuable land in return for $2,000 in money and merchandise and three sets of blacksmith's tools. The Choctaws also agreed to allow the United States to build a road from Natchez to Nashville in return for reaffirmation of the eastern boundary of the nation, settled in treaties with the English in 1765. Motivation for signing this first of many such cessions was based on economic pressure, political pressure

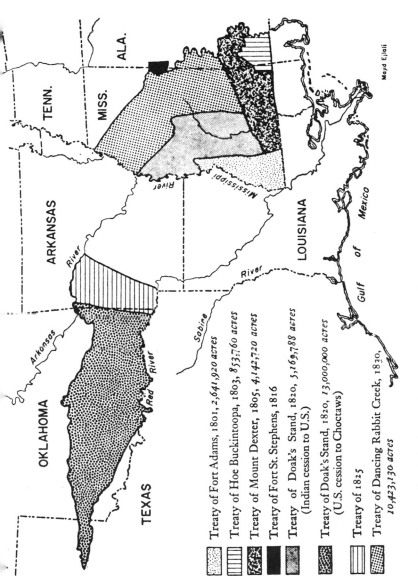

Map 2. Choctaw Land Cessions. From Arthur H. DeRosier, Jr. *The Removal of the Choctaw Indians* [70]. Reprinted by permission of the University of Tennessee Press.

Treaty of Fort Adams, 1801, *2,641,920 acres*

Treaty of Hoe Buckintoopa, 1803, *853,760 acres*

Treaty of Mount Dexter, 1805, *4,142,720 acres*

Treaty of Fort St. Stephens, 1816

Treaty of Doak's Stand, 1820, *5,169,788 acres* (Indian cession to U.S.)

Treaty of Doak's Stand, 1820, *13,000,000 acres* (U.S. cession to Choctaws)

Treaty of 1825

Treaty of Dancing Rabbit Creek, 1830, *10,423,130 acres*

Majid Ejlali

from Washington, and the Choctaw belief that the Treaty of Fort Adams would satiate the growing demands by settlers and the United States government for arable lands. Such was not to be the case, and the Choctaws were increasingly brought to the treaty-making table in the early nineteenth century to pay debts to American and European trading and land companies. All these treaties reveal the increased pressure not only upon the Choctaw Nation as a whole but upon its political structure as well. For the view that by 1805, the year associated with the First Choctaw Cession or the Treaty of Mount Dexter, the political leaders of the Choctaw districts had been corrupted by cash and other bonuses built into the treaties by United States officials, see Thelma V. Bounds, *Children of Nanih Waiya* [20].

The period from the cession of more than four million acres of prime farmland by the Choctaw chiefs in 1805 up to the Treaty of Doak's Stand of 1820, in which the Choctaws ceded five million additional acres of land in Mississippi in exchange for thirteen million acres of unfamiliar soil in present-day Arkansas and Oklahoma, was largely one of cooperation with the United States government. During the War of 1812 and during the Creek Wars between 1813 and 1815, many Choctaw warriors assisted the United States against the Creeks and aided in Andrew Jackson's defense of New Orleans against British invasion. The option for Pushmataha, a leading chief of the Choctaw in 1812 and a signatory of the treaty of 1805, was to ally with Tecumseh against the United States. The Choctaws chose not to commence hostilities against the United States, and when the Creeks defended themselves against the United States in 1813, Pushmataha sided with the Americans and provided Choctaw warriors for battle against the Creeks at Horseshoe Bend. For a sympathetic treatment of Pushmataha's actions as a leader of Choctaws and background events that eventually led to the signing of the Treaty of Doak's Stand in 1820, the legal agreement that paved the road for the removal of the Choctaw Nation to Indian Territory, see Arthur H. DeRosier, Jr.'s, excellent study *The Removal of the Choctaw Indians* [70]. Texts of Choctaw treaties can be found in Charles J. Kappler, *Indian Affairs: Laws and Treaties* [129], and in Charles Royce, *Indian Land Cessions in the United States* [196].

Serious scholars will want to consult Dunbar Rowland's *Mississippi Territorial Archives, 1798–1803* [193] and Clarence E. Carter's *The Territorial Papers of the United States,* volume 5, *The Territory of Mississippi, 1798–1817* [34] for the period 1783–1820. Together these constitute an essential body of official correspondence concerning these critical years of Choctaw relations with the citizenry and government of the United States. The *Annual Reports of the Commissioner of Indian Affairs* [215] should also be consulted.

In addition to treaty-making and subsequent land cessions, missionization greatly influenced the Choctaws in the first quarter of the nineteenth century. Although two Roman Catholic missions were established

among the people in the eighteenth century, these had
little effect in changing Choctaw culture and religion
[16]. By 1817 the Choctaws had been influenced by
many government agents and a growing population of
mixed-bloods, most of whom were the product of intermarriage between White traders and Choctaw wom-
en. And in that year the American Board of Commissioners for Foreign Missions established a "station"
among the Cherokees. Several White traders living
among the Choctaws saw not only opportunities to
educate their own mixed-blooded children, but a
chance for the Choctaws in general to gain the advan-
tages of reading and writing. Thus, in 1818, Cyrus
Kingsbury established a Presbyterian mission on the
Yalobusha River, beginning the process of effective
Christian proselytism among the Choctaw people. By
1820 Methodists and Baptists followed the lead of the
Presbyterians and entrenched themselves in Choctaw
country. The influence of missionaries, in tandem with
an Indian school program that resulted in thirteen
schools being built among the Choctaws by 1825,
changed much in Choctaw life and culture.

The most noticeable effect of missionization in the
period before removal to Indian Territory was altera-
tion of the traditional kinship system of the Choctaws.
Women's roles in a matrilineal society such as that of
the Choctaws were perceived by missionaries as con-
trary to Christian doctrine, where males are given dominant roles. Fred Eggan in "Historical Changes in the
Choctaw Kinship System" [77] perceptively analyzed

the important changes that accompanied acculturation under the mission "station" system. Particularly important for understanding culture change during this period was the change in land regulations and marital responsibilities. In traditional Choctaw culture women not only worked the fields but were totally responsible for their children's welfare and inheritance. The new system, which placed males in the dominant role as heads of households, added marriage laws whereby children inherited their father's estate. It also placed parental responsibility for maintainance of children upon their fathers, who in former times had been responsible only for their nephews. Eventually the mission system, combined with a growing mixed-blood population, eroded clan structure, which had traditionally served as a governing body. The new political order involved election of males from throughout the Choctaw district by male heads of households. Hereditary chieftainships that had formerly passed from uncle to nephew were now negated. Women were excluded from voting, and clans and moieties were sidestepped in the process of determining political leaders. Although clans survived as visible aspects of Choctaw culture after removal to Indian Territory, missionization and these accompanying deculturative changes served to undermine Choctaw social and political organization from 1819 forward.

Early missionary activities have been discussed in a number of articles, including William A. Love, "The Mayhew Mission to the Choctaws" [147]; Dawson A.

Phelps, "The Choctaw Mission: An Experiment in Civilization" [185]; William L. Hiemstra, "Early Presbyterian Missions among the Choctaw and Chickasaw Indians in Mississippi" [118]; and Arminta Scott Spalding, "From the Natchez Trace to Oklahoma: Development of Christian Civilization among the Choctaws, 1800–1860" [202]. Adam Hodgson, an Englishman who traveled through Choctaw country in 1820–21, described the mission and its influence upon Choctaw culture in his *Remarks during a Journey through North America* [122].

Although their efforts did much to alter traditional Choctaw culture, early missionaries contributed a great deal to our knowledge of the Choctaw people. Alfred Wright described some of their origin legends to readers of the *Missionary Herald* [226]. Cyrus Byington and Cyrus Kingsbury, founders of the first missions among the Choctaws, not only were interested in converting Indians to Christianity but also were interested in establishing model programs of boarding-school education for Indian youths under the sponsorship of the churches (in this case the Presbyterians) and the federal government. The theory behind such schools (duplicated elsewhere) was to take advantage of the United States Congress's 1818 decision to subsidize missionaries as part of the annuity payments agreed upon in treaties with American Indian tribes. With federal backing, the Presbyterians and other Protestant sects opened many schools in Choctaw communities and taught elementary courses in English, spelling, arithmetic, and religious instruction as well as vocational subjects. As more converts were made among the Choctaws (especially among the mixed-bloods), Byington found it essential to teach reading in the native language. He therefore compiled *A Dictionary of the Choctaw Language* [30] as well as a "Grammar of the Choctaw Language" [29]. He also translated hymns, the New Testament, a speller, and an almanac into Choctaw. A sketch of Byington's career can be found in Edward Burl Austin's "Cyrus Byington" [8]. Kingbury's life has recently been studied by Arminta Scott Spalding in "Cyrus Kingsbury: Missionary to the Choctaws" [203].

Both men were extremely influential in instilling in the Choctaws a pride in their educational system. By 1830 there were eleven schools in the Choctaw country, with twenty-nine teachers and two hundred and sixty students. Two hundred and fifty adults were also being taught to read in Choctaw under a separate program. Other Choctaws were attending the Choctaw academy for boys, located in Kentucky as a result of an agreement between the people and the Baptists. For a good summary of these educational institutions and the changes in Choctaw life that resulted from their various programs, see chapter 2 of Angie Debo, *The Rise and Fall of the Choctaw Republic* [59], Arthur H. DeRosier, Jr., *The Removal of the Choctaw Indians* [70], and Jesse O. McKee and Jon A. Schlenker, *The Choctaws: Cultural Evolution of a Native American Tribe* [151].

Choctaw Removal

Acculturative influences of missionaries and European-designed educational systems did not undermine Choctaw traditional social and political life single-handed. After gaining statehood in 1817, Mississippi asserted its new status in the Union by abolishing all tribal rights, privileges, and immunities enjoyed by Indians within the limits of the state. For the Choctaws, this edict caused enormous problems not only in their relationship with the state, but internally as well. By the mid-1820s the Choctaws had become excellent farmers by Euramerican standards. Deeply involved in the expanding cotton economy of the South, the Choctaws—from their point of view—had fully cooperated and had lived up to their obligations as outlined in treaties signed with the United States government. But cooperation and economic productivity were not enough for the state of Mississippi, whose legislators seized every available opportunity to reduce Choctaw prerogatives in the political and economic arenas of their changing life-style.

Choctaw removal in 1830, the events leading up to it, and its implications for other tribes throughout the East must be considered a watershed in the history of this tribe and neighboring tribes who were dispossessed and transported to Indian Territory. The decade 1820–30 is especially important in Choctaw tribal history in that the people became bitterly divided over whether to accept the offer of the United States government to exchange land in Mississippi for land west of the Mississippi River. The best general source concerning the political history of the Choctaws before 1830 is Robert S. Cotterill's *The Southern Indians: The Story of the Civilized Tribes before Removal* [52]. Cotterill's work is an excellent study of the complexities not only of the relationship of the southeastern tribes with the French, Spanish, and English and finally the United States, but also of the complex relationships among the tribes themselves. Angie Debo's *The Rise and Fall of the Choctaw Republic* [59] provides a useful summary of traditional Choctaw culture and events leading up to removal. This material, drawn mainly from the work of John R. Swanton [205, 207, 208, 209], is further enhanced by Debo's well-researched and detailed study of the removal period itself and of its consequences for the Choctaw tribe. Debo, better than any author before or since, puts into perspective the diplomatic relationship of the Choctaws with colonial European governments. She also successfully unravels the complex diplomatic history of Choctaw–United States relations in the period following the Treaty of Hopewell.

During the removal period, Choctaw culture came under strenuous attack both in Mississippi and in Indian Territory. From this point forward Choctaw history must be divided into those who remained in Mississippi and those who migrated to Indian Territory. On the eve of removal and during the process itself, Horatio B. Cushman, son of missionaries who spent most of their lives among the Choctaws in Mississippi, recorded and wrote an important work that sheds much light on this transitional period of the people. His *History of the Choctaw, Chickasaw and Natchez Indians* [56] demonstrates a strong Christian bias but is extremely valuable for its observations on the removal process. Cushman, as one of twin brothers, was considered by the Choctaws to be a specially gifted person who possessed special powers. As such, he and his brother were "borrowed" by the Choctaws to deal with a plague of locusts that was devastating the Choctaw cornfields. Throughout Cushman's account the reader will find essential notes on the Choctaws that are not divulged to other non-Choctaw writers. This information, set forth in his *History* as a summary of much oral history, may be considered an essential interpretation by a White of Choctaw perceptions of their own history during the removal period. Many events poorly documented elsewhere—such as the visit of the Shawnee chief Tecumseh in 1811 and his unsuccessful effort to persuade the Choctaws to join his confederacy against the United States during the War of 1812—are found in this volume.

Another interesting account that deals with the transition between the traditional Choctaw culture as it existed in Mississippi and as it adapted to the changing conditions imposed by missionary and educational activities and by removal is that by John Edwards, "The Choctaw Indians in the Middle of the Nineteenth Century" [75]. Edwards gathered his information among the Oklahoma Choctaws but contrasted it with the earlier customs remembered from Mississippi. His Christian bias obviously colored his interpretations of the significance of the culture changes he described. Choctaw life in Mississippi shortly before the bulk of the tribe had been removed was described briefly by John A. Watkins in "The Choctaws in Mississippi" [221]. In "A Contribution to Chacta History" [222], Watkins provided a description of an early Choctaw-Osage battle remembered by a member of the tribe. Since Watkins had gathered his materials directly from Choctaws in the early 1800s, his remarks are valuable as those of a direct observer of Choctaw life.

As we noted previously, in the period before removal the Choctaws ceded much of their land east of the Mississippi River in a series of treaties. The effect of those treaties was to begin a process of Choctaw removal even before 1830. "Indian Removal," a complex period in Indian-White relations, is often discussed without making distinct each tribe's peculiar history of events during these critical years. In the case of Choctaw removal, the reader is cautioned to avoid oversimplifying what was a very complex problem both for officials of the Choctaw Nation and for officials of the United States. The lands west of the Mississippi to which the Choctaw removed were not totally alien to the Choctaw before the 1820s. Many of these lands in present-day Arkansas and Oklahoma were traditional hunting grounds utilized by both the Choctaws and the Osages—hence the great rivalry between these two tribes. *The Removal of the Choctaw Indians* [70], by Arthur H. DeRosier, Jr., examines the complexities of removal, emphasizing the crucial roles of Thomas Jefferson, John C. Calhoun, and Andrew Jackson in the development and administration of removal policy. First suggested by Jefferson after the purchase of Louisiana, according to DeRosier removal was a debate that centered not on policy or ethics but on strategy and timing. In unraveling the political intrigues that eventually uprooted the majority of Choctaws from their Mississippi homeland, DeRosier paints an unflattering portrait of Jefferson, whose desire to deal equitably with Indians was compromised by his use of deception to acquire Choctaw lands. After the War of 1812 the United States placed great pressure upon the Choctaws to open their lands to White settlement. In 1820 the Treaty of Doak's Stand awarded the Choctaws some 13,000,000 acres in Arkansas and Oklahoma in return for 5,000,000 acres. They were expected to emigrate voluntarily. DeRosier fully appreciates the Choctaws' dilemma. His analysis of the negotiations at Dancing Rabbit Creek and of the hardships of removal is sympathetic. DeRosier has written a number of articles about Choctaw removal [64, 66, 67, 68, 69, 71]. His latest study, "The Choctaw Indians: Negotiations for Survival" [71], examines the Treaty of Doak's Stand and the Treaty of 1825, which revised the Choctaw and Arkansas border.

The United States established an agency at Fort Smith to handle the affairs of Choctaws who emigrated to Oklahoma after 1820. The activities of this agency are discussed by Edwin C. Bearss in his article "Fort Smith as the Agency for the Western Choctaws" [15]. Grant Foreman, whose knowledge of the Five Civilized Tribes remains unsurpassed, devotes the final chapter of *Indians and Pioneers* [86] to the problems the Choctaws faced in settling a new land and establishing harmonious relations with Plains Indians. He pursues these topics for the years 1830 to 1860 in *Advancing the Frontier* [88]. In the "Final Move of the Choctaws" [210], Rex Syndergaard describes the efforts of the United States to induce Choctaws to move voluntarily to Oklahoma in the years 1825 to 1830.

By 1829 about 150 Choctaws had moved to their new territory. It soon became apparent that few Choctaws were willing to emigrate. Federal officials became increasingly impatient with a policy of voluntary removal. Pressured by land-hungry Whites, in January 1830 the state of Mississippi presumptuously assumed jurisdiction in the matter and over Choctaw laws and abrogated tribal sovereignty. An important documentary source for these actions is the Mississippi state code [167]. In May, Congress finally took a position by passing the Indian Removal Act, which provided the president with the necessary sanctions and funding for the relocation of the eastern tribes. Choctaw removal, according to Ronald N. Satz in his important study, *American Indian Policy in the Jacksonian Era* [197], was a test case for the Jackson administration. In September, federal commissioners advised the Choctaws that their lands could not be protected from usurpation by the state of Mississippi. Succumbing to these tactics, the Choctaws consented to removal. The volatile situation at Dancing Rabbit Creek is depicted in two significant articles by Henry S. Halbert: "The Last Indian Council on Noxubee River" [113] and "Story of the Treaty of Dancing Rabbit" [114]. Halbert's articles add a poignant footnote to the story of removal.

Grant Foreman provides the basic study of the 1830s, when southern Indians were deprived of their patrimony and taken to Oklahoma. His *Indian Removal* [87] is a massive indictment of United States mismanagement of its trust. Contractors charged inflated prices and supplied inferior goods. Unscrupulous Whites preyed upon the emigrants. Cholera and other diseases ravaged the tribesmen, and thousands of Choctaws died. Muriel H. Wright, a historian of Choctaw descent, also describes the sufferings of this era in "The Removal of the Choctaws to the Indian Territory" [227]. George S. Gaines, who was commissioned by the United States to superintend Choctaw removal in Mississippi, defends his actions in "Removal of the Choctaws" [91]. In 1834 a report by the Commissary General of Subsistence, *Indian Removals: Correspondence on the Subject of the Emigration of Indians* [214], was published by the United States Senate. This report contains numerous documents of Choctaw removal. Occasionally the voices of individuals cry out from its pages and permit us to appreciate the human dimensions of their situation.

Biographies of certain Choctaw leaders who were

influential in the removal treaties negotiations provide interesting insight into the internal politics of the tribe. Anna Lewis's *Chief Pushmataha, American Patriot* [140] is an important study of this leader. Although not written in a scholarly manner, it is a good introduction to the removal period and its politics. Gideon Lincecum recorded the "Life of Apushimataha" [143] in about 1821, and Lewis drew heavily on Lincecum's biography. Mrs. N. D. Deupree's "Greenwood LeFlore" [72] is very complimentary to the subject, who negotiated the removal treaty, especially the fourteenth article, which provided for allotments for those who wished to remain in Mississippi. LeFlore himself did not make the move but remained behind in Mississippi to become an important southern planter, Allene DeShazo Smith's biography, *Greenwood LeFlore and the Choctaw Indians of the Mississippi Valley* [200], is another account of LeFlore's life, albeit a very uncritical one. A comprehensive biography of LeFlore is definitely needed. W. David Baird's biography, *Peter Pitchlynn: Chief of the Choctaws* [12], recounts the career of the son of John Pitchlynn, an influential White trader who had worked against the removal treaty. The United States had been authorized by the Treaty of Dancing Rabbit Creek to defray removal expenses by selling Choctaw lands in Mississippi and Alabama. The United States realized a profit of some $3,000,000 after removal costs were deducted, and the attempts of the Choctaws to recover this money became known as the "net proceeds claim." Peter Pitchlynn became the Choctaw official most involved with the recovery of the net proceeds. Baird depicts Pitchlynn as a man of abundant talents who was plagued by insecurities arising from his mixed heritage. His attachments were too weak to resist personal peculation. As a tribal delegate in Washington, D.C., he contracted the services of lobbyists and lawyers to expedite the Choctaw claims. Apparently he was guilty of accepting kickbacks from attorneys' fees. As a study of Choctaw fiscal and political affairs, Baird's biography is invaluable. Charles Lanman, who visited the Choctaws in 1870, gives a more sympathetic account of the former chief in his article, "Peter Pitchlynn" [136].

The removal of the majority of the Choctaw tribe to what is now the state of Oklahoma brought into focus the major crisis within the tribe. Those who wished to continue to live as members of the tribe necessarily had to move with the tribe to the lands west of the Mississippi River that had been guaranteed by the Treaty of Dancing Rabbit Creek. Those who wished to remain in the homeland, which represented the traditions of the tribe and which encompassed the sacred mound, Nanih Waiya, could do so by claiming individual lands. But the claims of those individuals were largely thwarted by the actions of the government agent, who refused to list claimants. In the end, the Choctaws who chose to remain in Mississippi became a landless people struggling to preserve their own sense of identity and traditions. Those who moved to Oklahoma were faced with the prospect of establishing a new source of identity. After 1830, then, the history of the Choctaws is that of two distinctive groups, associated by common memories but faced with very different life-styles.

A remarkable novel captures the essence of the identity of the Choctaw people. Its basis in historical fact can be found in the period during which certain of the Choctaws, under the pressure of treaties by which the tribe began ceding their lands east of the Mississippi River, gave up their attachment to the traditional homeland and moved into the western territory that they received in exchange for their eastern lands. *Okla Hannali* [135], by R. A. Lafferty, is the story of one such man, an extraordinary individual, as the people of the Sixtowns district of the Choctaw Nation had always been. Although told in fictional form, his story captures the cadence and flow of Choctaw speech. Certain customs of the tribe—for example, the habit of the Choctaw chucklers of breaking into laughter, chuckling at some shared but unspoken humor—are admirably portrayed. The story of Okla Hannali bridges the gap between the Oklahoma Choctaws and the Mississippi Choctaws, whose communities and identities are still distinctive in present society.

Choctaws in Indian Territory, 1830–1907

Although older geographical and political divisions were renewed, they were not as strong as before. Weakened by the loss of tribesmen who had chosen to stay in Mississippi, they suffered the residual effects of the removal crisis. Moreover, the mixed-bloods gravitated to the fertile soil of the Red and Arkansas river valleys, while the more conservative full-bloods moved into the mountainous eastern region. The Choctaws reconstituted their government, opened lands to cultivation and livestock, built towns and schools, and sank roots into a country that the United States promised never again to usurp.

Although some of its judgments need to be modified, the best study of Oklahoma Choctaw history is Debo's *Rise and Fall of the Choctaw Republic* [59]. She has a solid grasp of Choctaw politics, and her most telling insights concern the strategies of Choctaw politicians as they maneuvered to protect their nation's independence. She concludes her study with the merger of the Choctaws into the new state of Oklahoma in 1907. Very little of importance has escaped Debo's attention, and her work remains the point of departure for all subsequent Oklahoma Choctaw studies. Muriel H. Wright has an informative sketch of the Choctaws in her *Guide to the Indian Tribes of Oklahoma* [231]. Wright relates the history of the Choctaws from removal to the Civil War in her article "Brief Outline of the Choctaw and the Chickasaw Nations" [228]. Additional information on the Choctaws before 1860 may be found in Grant Foreman's *The Five Civilized Tribes* [89]. Removal had left the Choctaws demoralized and highly distrustful of the United States. Even the missionaries were objects of Choctaw suspicion. A series of major floods, drought, and disease combined to wreak havoc during the first years of settlement. By the 1840s, however, the Choctaws had embarked upon a remarkable program of economic and social development. Despite Foreman's tendency to accept missionary reports at face value, especially in regard to alcoholism, he provides a valuable introduction to the Choctaw adaptation to Oklahoma.

Choctaw adjustment to Oklahoma was hampered by population losses sustained during removal and by a continuing high mortality rate. Between 1830 and 1860 the tribe's numbers declined from 18,963 to 13,666, a loss of almost 28 percent. Cholera and smallpox were especially destructive. In her two-part study "Health Conditions in Indian Territory" [54, 55], Bernice Crockett examines the impact of disease from 1830 to 1890. Choctaw efforts to combat these diseases are described by Virginia R. Allen in "Medical Practices and Health in the Choctaw Nation, 1831–1885" [6]. Allen gives special attention to the *alikchi,* practitioners of traditional medicine. After the Civil War a number of Choctaws acquired formal training in modern medicine. By combining traditional and modern practices, the Choctaws developed a satisfactory level of medical treatment. In their article "Health and Medical Practice in the Choctaw Nation" [145], Wallace B. Love and R. Palmer Howard pay particular attention to the Choctaw Board of Health, which was established in 1884 and which developed uniform standards of medical treatment. The demographic history of the Choctaws is placed in perspective by Michael F. Doran's article "Population Statistics of Nineteenth Century Indian Territory" [73].

Choctaw relations with the United States after removal were mired in controversy. One of the most serious disputes involved the location of the eastern border of the nation. The treaty of 1825 established a boundary beginning 100 paces west of Fort Smith, Arkansas, and extending directly south to the Red River. When the federal surveyor adjusted the line to the southwest, the Choctaws were defrauded of 136,204.02 acres. Years of lobbying and litigation were required, as is made clear by W. David Baird in "Arkansas's Choctaw Boundary" [11], before the Court of Claims compensated the Choctaws in 1886. Additional information on this dispute may be found in an article by Joseph Stanley Clark, "The Eastern Boundary of Oklahoma" [45]. Despite the 1825 treaty line, the state of Arkansas asserted a border extending west to about present-day Muskogee. The treaty of 1855 called for a resurvey of the eastern boundary; but federal officials, succumbing to the pressure of Arkansas, merely retraced the 1825 line. In 1877 Congress appropriated funds for another survey, which determined that the border was indeed inaccurate. After repeated Choctaw attempts to gain compensation, Congress in 1881 permitted the tribe to bring suit in the Court of Claims. On 25 January 1886 this court awarded the Choctaws a judgment of $68,102 or 50¢ an acre.

After arriving in the West, the Choctaws quickly reestablished their government. They adapted their constitution to the new conditions, revised the legal code, and provided for courts and jails. All aspects of Choctaw legal and administrative history may be traced in the *Constitution and Laws of the Choctaw Nation* [37, 38]. These statutes were analyzed by Oliver Knight in "Fifty Years of Choctaw Law, 1834–1884" [133]. Muriel H. Wright describes the workings of local governing bodies in "Organization of Counties in the Choctaw and Chickasaw Nations" [229]. In 1837 the Chickasaws became a fourth district of the Choctaw Nation, but in 1855 they were permitted to separate and form their own government. However, the separation was not complete. The two tribes continued to share subsurface rights and mineral royalties. Negotiations with the United States were conducted jointly, and individuals could select allotments of land in either nation. The best study of Choctaw and Chickasaw relations is found in Arrell Gibson's *The Chickasaws* [92]. His book provides a valuable introduction to the general history of Indian Territory as well.

The United States managed its relations with the Choctaws through a superintendent of Indian affairs and through resident agents. Cheryl Haun Morris has compiled biographical sketches of these agents in her article "Choctaw and Chickasaw Indian Agents, 1831–1874" [169]. In a detailed study, "The Armstrongs of Indian Territory" [85], Carolyn Thomas Foreman provides information on the careers of two agents, the brothers Francis and William Armstrong. Serving as agent from 1832 to 1847, William Armstrong won the respect of the Choctaws and helped diminish their distrust of the federal government.

After a sluggish start, the Choctaws made a successful economic adjustment to Oklahoma. By the 1850s large quantities of cotton, timber, and other products were being exported down the Arkansas and Red rivers. Because Choctaw lands were held in common, any citizen could use as much as he desired as long as he did not infringe on his neighbors. This system permitted some of the Choctaws to appropriate hundreds of acres for personal gain. One such individual was Robert M. Jones, who reportedly owned more then five hundred Black slaves, two steamboats, several plantations, and banks in Texas and in Indian Territory. Jones later represented the Choctaws and Chickasaws in the Confederate Congress. Jones's career is briefly summarized in T. Paul Wilson's article "Delegates of the Five Civilized Tribes to the Confederate Congress" [224]. Norman Arthur Graebner has analyzed this communal land system in "The Public Land Policy of the Five Civilized Tribes" [98]. After the Civil War, certain restrictions were placed on the use of pasture and mineral lands. Graebner assesses the difficulties the Choctaw emigrants faced in adjusting to the soil and climatic conditions of Oklahoma in his article "Pioneer Indian Agriculture in Oklahoma" [97].

The principal commercial crop of the Choctaws was cotton. The importance of this item is discussed by Gilbert C. Fite in "Development of the Cotton Industry by the Five Civilized Tribes in Indian Territory" [79]. Michael F. Doran argues that cattle raising was the most important industry in Indian Territory in his article "Antebellum Cattle Herding in the Indian Territory" [74]. Doran presents evidence that Indian ranchers sold at least 100,000 head of cattle before the Civil War to buyers in Arkansas and Missouri and to emigrants on the California Road. Laura Baum Graebner's study "Agriculture among the Five Civilized Tribes, 1840–1906" [96] is a superb overview of the tribes' agricultural achievements.

Contemporary observers were favorably impressed by Choctaw economic progress and by the resilience of their spirit. Baldwin Möllhausen, a German artist who accompanied the Whipple Survey of 1853 as a topographer, praises the agricultural skills of the Choctaws and their public decorum in a memoir that has been partially reprinted by Muriel H. Wright and George H. Shirk in "Artist Möllhausen in Oklahoma" [233]. In addition to his paintings, George Catlin left a sympathetic description of Choctaw society in his *Letters and Notes of the Manners, Customs and Condition of the North American Indians* [35]. Much information about the Choctaws is given in volumes 4 and 5 of Henry Rowe Schoolcraft's *Archives of Aboriginal Knowledge* [198]. Additional testimony concerning Choctaw life may be found in contemporary newspapers. The *Choctaw Telegraph,* started in 1842, was the first newspaper published in the Choctaw Nation. James D. Morrison analyzes its content in his article "News for the Choctaws" [170]. An annotated list of all newspapers published in the Choctaw Nation from 1842 to 1907 is presented by Carolyn T. Foreman in her book *Oklahoma Imprints 1835–1907* [83].

The Choctaws had placed a high value on education in Mississippi, a tradition repeated after removal to the West. As we mentioned earlier, by removal eleven schools had been established in Mississippi, with twenty-nine teachers and two hundred and sixty students. Eighty-nine additional students were enrolled at Colonel Richard Johnson's Choctaw Academy in Kentucky. The history of this remarkable institution, which served the Choctaws until 1846, is told by Carolyn Foreman in a series of articles entitled "The Choctaw Academy" [80, 81, 82]. An earlier evaluation of this school is by Mrs. Shelley D. Rouse, "Colonel Dick Johnson's Choctaw Academy" [192]. Ethel McMillan provides another perspective in her "First National Indian School" [156].

After removal the Choctaws embarked on a program of comprehensive education. By the early 1840s they were operating a system of neighborhood schools and were planning a number of boarding schools. Instruction was in both Choctaw and English. Adult education was provided on weekends and evenings. Scholarships were awarded to students who desired to attend American colleges and universities. A recent dissertation by Eloise G. Spear is an admirable synthesis of Choctaw educational achievements [204]. She traces the history of Choctaw education from 1831, when a denominational school was established by the Presbyterians at Wheelock Mission, to the 1870s. Correspondence between Washington, D.C., and these various schools is found in "About Some of Our First Schools in Choctaw Nation" [25], edited by J. Y. Bryce.

The most important landmark in the development of a tribal school system was the Education Act of 1842, which created a board of trustees and authorized the construction of two boarding schools. Spencer Academy was soon opened for boys, and New Hope Seminary was later established for girls. W. David Baird relates the history of Spencer Academy from 1842 to 1900 [10], and Carolyn Thomas Foreman makes a similar study in her "New Hope Seminary" [84]. William L. Hiemstra discusses the educational work during 1845 to 1861 in "Presbyterian Mission Schools among the Choctaws and Chickasaws" [120].

Choctaw educational progress was halted by the Civil War, when schools were closed for most of the war period. Funds and teachers were difficult to obtain in the postwar years, but by the late 1860s the Choctaws were again committed to education. The scope of Choctaw schooling after the war is clearly explained by Angie Debo in "Education in the Choctaw Country after the Civil War" [58]. As more Choctaws became qualified, the nation relied less on missionary organizations for teachers. In 1884 attendance in the neighborhood schools became compulsory. Segregated schools were established for the freedmen. In the school year 1892–93, 4,329 students attended 189 neighborhood schools and 7 boarding schools, and 40 students were enrolled in American colleges on tribal scholarships. As a prelude to Oklahoma's statehood, the Choctaw schools were taken over by the United States in 1899. In 1907 they were merged into the school system of the state of Oklahoma.

The Choctaws in Oklahoma continued to be influenced by Protestant missionaries. By the 1850s, approximately 25 percent of the tribe were Christian converts, and a handful had themselves become ministers. The missionaries served as teachers, nurses, and agricultural agents; and they became involved in social and political issues. Their advice was sought by the Choctaws during the removal crisis, and they were soon drawn into the debate over slavery. The Presbyterian mission among the Choctaws has been the subject of much scholarship. Its labors before the Civil War are discussed by William Hiemstra in his article "Presbyterian Missionaries and Mission Churches among the Choctaw and Chickasaw Indians" [119]. His work is complemented by Natalie Morrison Denison's study "Missions and Missionaries of the Presbyterian Church, U.S., among the Choctaws" [62], which deals with the years after 1865. By far the best study of Presbyterian work among the Choctaws is the dissertation by Michael Christopher Coleman, "Presbyterian Missionaries and Their Attitudes to the American Indians, 1837–1893" [48]. Coleman makes an intensive study of the careers of thirteen missionaries who lived among the Oklahoma Choctaws and the Nez Perce of the Pacific Northwest. William B. Morrison has outlined the work of the Presbyterian mission in *The Red Man's Trail* [175]. Morrison's book contains important facts about Presbyterian mission work, but it is often impressionistic and ethnocentric. The same author has written "The Choctaw Mission of the American Board of Commissioners for Foreign Missions" [174], an article touching upon aspects of the American Board's activities among the Choctaws in Mississippi and in Indian Territory.

The memoirs, diaries, and letters of the missionaries constitute an important source of Choctaw history. Isaac McCoy left a fascinating personal narrative of Baptist attempts to establish missions in Indian Territory in his book *History of Baptist Indian Missions* [148]. Two Methodist missionaries wrote at length about their service in the Choctaw Nation. William Henry Goode, superintendent of Fort Coffee Academy, left an account of this in *Outposts of Zion* [95]. The Reverend Henry C. Benson, a colleague of Goode's at Fort Coffee, described his work in *Life among the Choctaw Indians* [17]. Both men lived among the Choctaws from the early 1840s to the Civil War, and their books are revealing studies of the activities of the missionaries. In 1844 N. Sayre Harris, an inspector for the Protestant Episcopal church, visited the Choctaw Nation, and a portion of his journal is reprinted by Kenny R. Franks in his article "Missionaries in the West" [90]. Charles C. Copeland, a Presbyterian minister at Stockbridge mission, gives a pessimistic view of the future of the Choctaws in "Letter Mailed from Eagle Town, Choctaw Nation, 1842" [51].

The Choctaws and the missionaries could not avoid the debate over Black slavery. By the 1840s slave ownership was an integral aspect of Choctaw life. Although no more than 600, or 4 percent, of the Choctaws owned slaves, they had a disproportionate influence on the Choctaw government and economy. An elaborate slave code determined the relations between slaves and masters. Wyatt F. Jeltz's article "The Relations of Negroes and Choctaw and Chickasaw Indians" [128] places the development of Choctaw slavery in historical perspective. The anomalous nature of slaveholding among the Choctaws is discussed by C. Calvin Smith in his article "The Oppressed Oppressors: Negro Slavery among the Choctaw Indians of Oklahoma" [201]. Daniel F. Littlefield and Mary Littlefield describe the situation of free Blacks in the Choctaw Nation in their study "The Beams Family" [144]. William G. McLoughlin explores the relationship between Choctaw slavery and United States economic and racial policies in his article "Red Indians, Black Slavery and White Racism" [155]. McLoughlin's evaluations of mission work are exceptionally thoughtful.

Slavery was a deeply troubling issue for the missionaries. If they espoused abolition, they offended powerful Choctaw slaveholders whose support they needed to maintain their missions. But if they did not speak out against slavery, they abetted its success. Their dilemma is clearly explained by Robert T. Lewitt in his study "Indian Missions and Antislavery Sentiment" [141]. As early as the 1820s the American Board was troubled by the conflicting needs of mission work among the Indians and of opposition to slavery. Its response is discussed by Arthur H. DeRosier, Jr., in his article "Pioneers with Conflicting Ideals: Christianity and Slavery in the Choctaw Nation" [65]. William G. McLoughlin examines the reaction of the Presbyterian Board of Foreign Missions to slavery in "Indian Slaveholders and Presbyterian Missionaries, 1837–1861" [153].

Choctaw relations with the mission groups deteriorated as the debate over slavery became more acerbic. In 1859 the American Board abandoned its mission in the Indian Territory. Cyrus Kingsbury and others who had worked for years among the Choctaws elected to resign and continued their labors by affiliating with the Presbyterian Board of Home Missions. Kingsbury's son John portrays the strained relations between the Choctaws and the American Board in letters edited by James D. Morrison, "Note on Abolitionism in the Choctaw Nation" [173]. In "The Choctaw Slave-Burning" [154], William G. McLoughlin relates an incident that affected the decision of the American Board to withdraw from the nation. In 1859 a prominent Choctaw, Richard Harkins, was murdered. Believing that a Black woman had instigated the murder, a Choctaw mob burned her at the stake. Horrified by this brutality, the American Board began to reevaluate its mission to the Choctaws. As the Civil War neared, the missionaries became apprehensive about their safety. Their forebodings are shown in an article by William L. Hiemstra, "Presbyterian Missions among Choctaw and Chickasaw Indians, 1860–1861" [121]. Sue McBeth, a teacher at the mission school at Goodwater, depicts prewar conditions in her "Letters regarding Choctaw Missions and Missionaries," prepared for publication by Anna Lewis [139]. John Edwards describes his hurried departure from the Choctaw Nation in "An Account of My Escape from the South in 1861" [76]. His memoir is enhanced by the annotations of Muriel H. Wright.

Despite the initial opposition of Peter Pitchlynn and Principal Chief George Hudson, the Choctaw Nation signed a treaty with the Confederacy on 12 July 1861. The decision to do so was virtually unanimous, and the Choctaws thereby escaped the bitter factional disputes that ravaged the Seminoles, Creeks, and Cherokees during the war. The Choctaws and Chickasaws raised three regiments that saw service in Arkansas and in the Creek and Cherokee nations, but they were used primarily for home defense. The Choctaws experienced severe economic and social dislocations. Their schools were closed, buildings and crops destroyed, and livestock stolen. More than 6,000 Confederate Indians were maintained in camps along the Kiamichi, Blue, and Boggy rivers. Paul Bonnifield, in his article "The Choctaw Nation on the Eve of the Civil War" [18], emphasizes the significance of the constitutional changes of 1859 and 1860 and the attempt by various American corporations and politicians to turn Indian Territory into a state. The most thorough study of conditions in the Indian Territory during the war is Annie Heloise Abel's three-volume history *The American Indian as Slaveholder and Secessionist* [1, 2, 3]. Despite the title of her third volume, *The American Indian under*

Reconstruction, she deals only slightly with postwar social and economic conditions. Abel concludes her work with a discussion of the treaties signed in 1866 by the Choctaws and other Oklahoma tribes. The military participation of the Choctaws in the Civil War is placed in perspective by Lary C. and Donald A. Rampp in their book *The Civil War in the Indian Territory* [188]. The career of Douglas Cooper, agent to the Choctaws in the 1850s and commander of Choctaw and Chickasaw troops during the war, is traced in an excellent article by Muriel H. Wright, "General Douglas H. Cooper, C.S.A." [232]. Until his death in 1879, Cooper's fortunes were closely tied to the Choctaw Nation as he served as a lobbyist in Washington, D.C. James F. Morgan assesses the fiscal policy of the Choctaw Nation during the war in his study "The Choctaw Warrants of 1863" [168]. Once it became clear that the Confederacy could not provide specie payments, the Choctaws printed their own money, yet managed to escape the ruinous inflation that plagued various state governments during and after the war.

The Choctaws emerged from the war faced with an enormous task of reconstruction. Their financial resources were depleted, their economy had come to a virtual halt, and they had to make terms with the United States. The endeavors of the Choctaws to deal with these problems and their general progress after the war is related by James D. Morrison in his dissertation, "Social History of the Choctaw, 1865–1907" [171]. Morrison summarizes his findings in an article,

"Problems in the Industrial Progress of the Choctaw Nation, 1865–1907" [172]. The political history of the Choctaws from the Civil War to statehood in 1907 may be traced in a number of biographical sketches of the principal chiefs of the nation written by John Bartlett Meserve [161, 162, 163, 164, 165]. Peter James Hudson, a member of a prominent Choctaw family, gives an overview of Choctaw leadership in his article "A Story of Choctaw Chiefs" [127]. The careers of these officials attest to the vigor of Choctaw political institutions and to the difficulties of their position during years of continuous turmoil.

The United States and the Choctaws concluded a treaty early in 1866, after prolonged and difficult negotiations. The terms of this treaty are discussed by Marion Ray McCuller in his article "The Choctaw-Chickasaw Reconstruction Treaty of 1866" [149]. The United States agreed to restore all prewar trust funds, including the net proceeds award. The two tribes agreed to abolish slavery and to cede the western portion of their territory for $300,000, contingent upon their admitting the freedmen to citizenship. If they did not adopt the Blacks within two years, the United States would use the funds to relocate the freedmen. Their legal status remained unclear for years, however, when the United States did not remove the Blacks as the tribes requested. On 21 May 1883 the Choctaws finally adopted their former slaves but maintained a social separation of the races. Moreover, they denied the Blacks certain economic and legal rights. This subject is treated by Thomas F. Andrews in his article "Freedmen in Indian Territory" [7]. Lewis Anthony Kensell also discusses the situation of the freedmen in "Phases of Reconstruction in the Choctaw Nation, 1865–1870" [131]. Choctaw relations with the freedmen and other aspects of reconstruction are given extensive treatment by M. Thomas Bailey in *Reconstruction in Indian Territory* [9], a valuable synthesis of the history of the Five Tribes from 1865 to 1876.

The most serious political problem the Choctaws confronted after the Civil War was the demand by American economic interests to dissolve the tribal governments of Indian Territory and to open the territory's resources to Whites. The erosion and dissolution of Indian sovereignty is clearly told by H. Craig Miner in *The Corporation and the Indian* [166]. By the end of the nineteenth century, much of the wealth of Indian Territory was controlled by powerful railroad, livestock, coal, and oil companies. The interests of these corporations were supported by the policies of Indian reform groups that wanted the Indians' system of communal landholdings abolished and a system of private land usage substituted. Only under the latter system, so the reformers believed, would the Indians make progress in civilized ways. Responding to these pressures, the United States ultimately terminated all tribal governments in Indian Territory. The Indian governments, too weak to put up an effective resistance, were not innocent victims. As Miner points out, their policies encouraged corporate investment in tribal resources.

He is most impressive in his discussion of the actions of tribal politicians as they attempted to reconcile the often conflicting demands of economic development and tribal sovereignty.

Much of the pressure to abolish the Choctaw government emanated from railroad companies. By the treaty of 1866 the Choctaws were required to grant rights of way to one east-west and to one north-south railway. Shortly after the treaty was ratified, the Congress gave land grants involving millions of acres in Indian Territory to these companies contingent on the abolition of the tribal governments. The first railroad to be completed through the Choctaw Nation was the Missouri, Kansas and Texas, in January 1873. The history of its construction is told by Vincent V. Masterson in *The Katy Railroad and the Last Frontier* [158]. The Supreme Court later permitted additional railroads to enter Indian Territory, under the presumption that eminent domain rested with the United States. These companies soon clamored for land grants as well. This decision severely undermined Choctaw sovereignty. The economic interests of the Katy and other railway companies in Indian Territory were opposed to those of the Choctaws, and they persistently agitated for the termination of the Choctaw government. By 1902 six railroad companies had laid 780 miles of track in the Choctaw Nation.

Another industry that attracted American investors to the Choctaw Nation was coal mining. A coal boom began in that region in the 1880s, and by 1901 thirty-nine coal corporations were operating in the Choctaw country, employing 4,600 noncitizen miners and extracting almost 1.5 million tons of coal a year. In 1890 the Choctaws were paid $57,839 in coal royalties, and these revenues would reach well over $200,000 a year by statehood. Mining resulted in many social problems among the Choctaws. Such towns as Krebs and McAlester were populated largely by Whites, many of them recent European immigrants. The origins of this coal mining population are traced by Joseph Stanley Clark in his article "Immigrants in the Choctaw Coal Industry" [46]. In these towns law and order were difficult to maintain, prohibition laws were easily evaded, and prostitution flourished. Newspapers advocated that Whites should not be subject to "Indian laws" and lobbied for federal control and statehood. In 1894 a strike in the Choctaw coalfields was crushed by federal troops. To a large degree the development of the Choctaw coal resources was prompted by J. J. McAlester, an intermarried citizen of mixed Choctaw and Chickasaw background. McAlester is the subject of "An Oklahoma Indian Trader as a Frontiersman of Commerce" [134], by Oliver Knight. Much information about the growth of the coal industry in the Choctaw Nation is found in a dissertation by Gene Aldrich, "A History of the Coal Industry in Oklahoma to 1907" [5].

In 1893 the United States created a Commission to the Five Civilized Tribes, headed by Henry L. Dawes, former chairman of the Senate Committee on Indian Affairs. Its purpose was to persuade the tribes of Indian Territory to terminate their governments and to accept individual allotments of land. A convenient statistical and historical summary of the Choctaws at this time is presented by the U.S. Census Office, *Extra Census Bulletin: The Five Civilized Tribes in Indian Territory* [213]. The work of the Dawes Commission from 1893 to 1898 is described by Loren N. Brown in his article "The Dawes Commission" [22]. Brown deals specifically with the Choctaws in his articles "The Choctaw-Chickasaw Court Citizens" [23], concerning the problems of establishing tribal rolls, and "The Appraisal of the Lands of the Choctaws and Chickasaws" [24]. A contemporary report of the situation in Indian Territory was made by Charles F. Meserve of the Indian Rights Association, who published *The Dawes Commission and the Five Civilized Tribes of the Indian Territory* [160]. Meserve disparages the abilities of the Indians and unreservedly supports the efforts of the commission. A general treatment of the forces that led to statehood is made by Roy Gittinger in *The Formation of the State of Oklahoma* [94]. Gittinger traces the history of this movement from 1803 to 1906, but he emphasizes the pressures placed on the Indian nations by the boomer societies of the 1880s and by railways and other corporations.

At first the Choctaws were opposed to the purposes of the Dawes Commission, but a vigorous minority soon emerged, led by Green McCurtain, that urged the necessity of negotiation. McCurtain feared that if the Choctaws did not agree to terms, the United States would impose a mandatory settlement upon the tribe.

He was elected principal chief in 1896 and proceeded to negotiate the Atoka Agreement of 27 April 1897. By its terms the Choctaw Nation would come to an end, and each member would receive an equal share in the tribal domain. This agreement, though approved by the Choctaws, was rejected by Chickasaw voters. McCurtain's fears were realized in June 1898, when Congress passed the Curtis Act. Without Indian consent, the United States terminated all governments in the Indian Territory and mandated allotment in severalty. The tribes were given two years in which to negotiate suitable terms. The Choctaws accepted a settlement based upon the provisions of the Atoka Agreement and later refined by the Supplementary Agreement of 1902. Regulations for the allotment of land were specified, a citizenship court was created, and the sale of mineral lands within three years was authorized. The Dawes Commission drew up a tribal roll consisting of 18,981 Oklahoma Choctaws, 5,994 freedmen and their descendants, and 1,639 Choctaws recently arrived from Mississippi, all eligible for the distribution of Choctaw resources. The commission began to issue allotments in 1903. Each Choctaw citizen was assigned the equivalent of 320 acres of average land to be held in trust for twenty-one years. Since nineteen categories of land value were established, Choctaws could receive allotments ranging from 160 to 4,165 acres. Freedmen were eligible for only 40 acres of average land. In 1901 the Choctaws were granted American citizenship.

The reaction of the Choctaw people to this crisis is

reflected in the acts and resolutions that their tribal council passed in the years 1897 to 1904 [39, 40, 41, 42, 43]. They joined with Indians from other tribes to mitigate the impact of the Curtis Act. Such emigration companies as the Four Mothers Society wanted to liquidate the tribal domain immediately and use the funds to resettle in Mexico or South America. This desire to emigrate persisted into the 1930s. In the summer of 1905 the Choctaws sent representatives to a convention held in Muskogee to promote the admission of Indian Territory as a state separate from Oklahoma Territory. Amos Maxwell discusses the participation of Indian leaders in his article "The Sequoyah Convention" [159]. The proposed constitution of the state of Sequoyah was ignored by Theodore Roosevelt's administration, however, and Indian Territory was merged with Oklahoma Territory to form the new state of Oklahoma on 16 November 1907.

Choctaws of Oklahoma, 1907 to the Present

Since 1907 the Choctaw Nation has had only a tenuous existence. Because much of the work of the Dawes Commission had not been completed, Congress passed the Five Tribes Act of 1906, authorizing the president to appoint the principal chief of the Choctaws and other tribal officers. Green McCurtain, whose job had been to supervise the dissolution of Choctaw autonomy, continued to serve as principal chief until his death in 1910. At this time nearly two million acres of unallotted timber land and segregated coal and asphalt lands remained in tribal possession. Tribal royalties continued to accrue. Since 1910, chiefs appointed by the president have been Victor M. Locke, Jr., William F. Semple, William H. Harrison, Eliphalet N. Wright, Ben Dwight, William A. Durant, and Harry J. W. Belvin. The Choctaw tribal council continued to meet until 1911. After that date, ad hoc conventions were called upon the initiative of the principal chief. In 1934, an advisory council to the principal chief was created.

Very little has been written about the Choctaws since statehood. Brief introductions to this history are contained in the final section of W. David Baird's *The Choctaw People* [13] and in Muriel H. Wright's *Guide to the Indian Tribes of Oklahoma* [231]. Additional information may be found in Wright's study of her father, "A Brief Review of the Life of Doctor Eliphalet Nott Wright" [230]. Wright was the principal chief of the Choctaws from 1929 to his death in 1932. The most powerful description of the experience of the Choctaws and other tribes in Oklahoma is Angie Debo's book *And Still the Waters Run* [60]. Hers is a revealing and damning study of the negligence of the United States in the supervision of its trust. Debo begins her analysis with the 1890s and takes it to 1940. Statehood came as a crushing blow to the tribes of Indian Territory. They surrendered to the inevitable only after prolonged negotiations, with the threat of force always in the background. Their economic and social absorption into the new state, she makes painfully clear, was realized at a terrible and unregarded cost in human suffering.

Debo marshals considerable evidence that the

United States did not properly supervise the affairs of the Five Tribes. Much of what happened was the result not only of negligence, but of cupidity, fraud, and violence. The system of guardianship developed by the Congress in 1908 was especially susceptible to the manipulations of the venal. Passed over the objections of most Oklahoma Indians and the Office of Indian Affairs, this act turned over to the county courts the appointment of guardians for Indian minors and incompetents. Restrictions on the landholding of intermarried Whites, freedmen, and tribesmen of less than one-half blood were removed. Although a system of federal probate inspectors was created by this act, their numbers were so few that they had little influence. In ensuing years the lands of the restricted and unrestricted alike were exploited on a massive scale. Although many Choctaws were successful in the economic and political life of the state, by the 1930s most of them had been stripped of their resources and had become impoverished.

On 26 June 1938, Congress passed the Oklahoma Indian Welfare Act, which made Oklahoma tribes eligible for certain federal programs. Efforts of the federal government and of the state of Oklahoma held out hope for indigent Choctaw communities during the remainder of that decade. These years are depicted by B. T. Quinten in his article "Oklahoma Tribes, the Great Depression and the Indian Bureau" [187]. Despite the gains of the 1930s and 1940s, however, unemployment remained high among the Choctaws. A

major consequence of the Depression was an emigration of Choctaws to find jobs elsewhere. Hundreds of
Choctaws moved, especially to California, following the
cotton culture in which they were so experienced.
World War II induced other Choctaws to work in war
plants in California and elsewhere. In the 1950s the
federal program of relocation transplanted additional
hundreds to such cities as Dallas and Los Angeles, as
well as to Oklahoma City and Tulsa. Few studies have
been made of Choctaws living outside the boundaries
of the old Choctaw Nation.

In 1949 Angie Debo conducted a survey for the
Indian Rights Association, *The Five Civilized Tribes of Oklahoma* [61], showing that the Five Tribes had lost
nearly 90 percent of their land after 1907, dropping
from 20 million to 1,257,768 acres. A summary of this
report is found in the preface to the reprinted edition
of *And Still the Waters Run*. In that same year the Choctaws received per capita payments of $350, originating
in the purchase the previous year by Congress of all
remaining coal and asphalt lands for $8,500,000.
Theodore Roosevelt's administration had been unwill-
ing to sell these lands under the terms of the Supplementary Agreement of 1902 because much of this land
had been tied up in thirty-year leases. The Five Tribes
Act of 1906 had withdrawn these lands until the expi-
ration of the leases, but depressed prices in the 1920s
and 1930s had prevented their sale. In 1971 Debo
made yet another survey of conditions in Oklahoma,
indicating that lands continued to be lost at an appal-

ling rate. In this year the Five Tribes held 39,246 acres of tribal land, and individual allottees or their heirs retained only 574,190 acres.

Since the 1950s the Choctaws have weathered a termination crisis and have entered a period of recovery. In 1959 Congress passed an act that, if implemented, would have abolished the Choctaw government and dissolved all trust funds. With the support of Congressman Carl Albert, the Choctaws were able to effect the repeal of this act in 1971. In that same year Congress approved an act permitting the Five Tribes to elect their leaders. Under principal chiefs J. W. Belvin, David Gardner, and Hollis Roberts, all elected since 1971, the Choctaws have embarked upon a number of educational and industrial projects. They have constructed health centers and a hospital, opened a cultural center near Hugo, and developed a 2,600-acre cattle ranch near Tuskahoma. A tribal housing project has been started with funds initially provided in 1964 by the Office of Economic Opportunity. The Choctaws publish a tribal newspaper, *Bishinik* [44], which is the best source for contemporary events. Tribal offices are maintained in Durant, in buildings formerly belonging to the Oklahoma Presbyterian College.

In 1970 the Choctaws won a favorable judgment against the state of Oklahoma concerning the Arkansas River. In 1946 Congress had authorized a $1.2 billion project to dredge and dam the Arkansas. These actions changed the river's course, created a series of lakes, and permitted Tulsa to become an ocean port. In 1966 the Cherokees filed suit for damages, soon joined by the Chickasaws and Choctaws. They claimed that the riverbed and all dry lands exposed by the changing course of the river belonged to the tribes, since they had never been allotted to tribal members or purchased by the United States. Although the United States District Court for Eastern Oklahoma and the Tenth Circuit Court of Appeals ruled against the tribes, the Supreme Court upheld their contentions (*Choctaw Nation v. Oklahoma,* 397 U.S. 620–40). In 1973, after the Interior Department estimated the value of the riverbed and dry lands at $177,000,000, Congress authorized the department to litigate or arbitrate a settlement. The future lease or purchase of these resources also had to be negotiated. A summary of this case is found in Michael M. Gibson's article "Indian Claims in the Beds of Oklahoma Watercourses" [93]. With income eventually derived from this settlement and from other sources, it is to be expected that Choctaws will continue to be distinctive participants in the economic and social life of Oklahoma.

Choctaws in Mississippi and Louisiana

After the removal of the majority of the tribe to Indian Territory during the early 1830s, approximately 2,000 Choctaws remained behind in Mississippi. Many of them intended to file for individual allotments as guaranteed in Article 14 of the Treaty of Dancing Rabbit Creek. But government corruption (primarily in

the form of the Choctaw agent James Ward, who refused to register most of the Choctaw claims), the
influences of land speculators, and their own lack of
awareness of their situation (some simply did not know
about their rights to register or neglected to exercise
them), conspired to strip most of them of their rights
to land in Mississippi. The subsequent attempts of the
state of Mississippi to put pressure on the remaining
Choctaws within its boundaries to remove, and the attempts of the Choctaws to assert their rights to land
within the state, are documented in Franklin L. Riley's
article "Choctaw Land Claims" [189]. Edward Davis, in
"The Mississippi Choctaw," also deals with pressures
put on the Choctaw by the state of Mississippi and the
United States government to follow their kinspeople to
Indian Territory [57]. The federal government finally
offered land scrip to be redeemed from public lands
east of the Mississippi, but the scrip became the object
of land speculators. Mary Elizabeth Young's excellent
study *Redskins, Ruffleshirts and Rednecks: Indian
Allotments in Alabama and Mississippi 1830–1860* [234]
documents the process that reduced the Choctaws in
Mississippi by and large to the status of landless squat-
ters. Using land office records and government documents, Young studied the activities of major land companies to show how they aided the passage of Choctaw
lands into the hands of speculators. George D. Harmon
gives special attention to the methods by which land
companies exploited the Choctaws during 1831 to 1845
in his *Sixty Years of Indian Affairs* [116].

Deprived of land, most of the Choctaws in Mississippi faded quietly into the swamplands and largely vanished from the historical and ethnographic literature. From 1830 until 1918, when the federal government became aware of the poverty of their conditions and purchased land for them, these people were not legally recognized as an Indian tribe. Their culture and sense of identity, however, set them off from both Blacks and Whites in the South, and their anomalous position in the system of strict racial segregation in the South isolated them from significant contact with both Blacks and Whites. The history of the Mississippi Choctaws can only be pieced together from scattered sources. One of the major sources is the work of Henry S. Halbert, who was a teacher in the Catholic school at Tucker during the late 1800s. Halbert learned the Choctaw language, and he collected and recorded many oral traditions and extensively explored the Choctaw territory in Mississippi. He was thus the major recorder of the persistence of Choctaw identity in Mississippi. His numerous articles covered many aspects of traditional Choctaw life and history—"Funeral Customs of the Mississippi Choctaws" [109], "Courtship and Marriage among the Choctaws of Mississippi" [100], "The Choctaw Achahpih (Chungkee) Game" [101], "District Divisions of the Choctaw Nation" [111], "Okla Hannali; or, The Six Towns District of the Choctaws" [103], and "Pyramid and Old Road in Mississippi" [102]. Halbert's attempts to determine precisely the boundaries of ancient Choctaw towns and districts are a valuable re-creation of the historical situation of the Choctaws in Mississippi. His accounts of Choctaw life in the late nineteenth century, the only source of such information, are included in his reports on the Choctaw schools in the *Biennial Reports* of the Mississippi superintendent of schools [105, 106, 107, 110]. These reports and his accounts of historic places and events provide a sense of the continuity of Choctaw identity in Mississippi throughout the late 1800s and early 1900s. Halbert's article "Origin of Mashulaville" [115] and William A. Love's article "Mingo Moshulitubbee's Prairie Village" [146] provide a link between the Choctaws of 1830 and those communities that persisted in Mississippi.

Frances Densmore, in her usual thorough fashion, studied Choctaw music in Mississippi in the early 1930s, including brief notes on the customs surrounding the singing of the songs she recorded [63]. Some of the Choctaws had migrated to other places in the South after the removal period, and David I. Bushnell, Jr., recorded details of Choctaw life in Louisiana in *The Choctaw of Bayou Lacomb St. Tammany Parish Louisiana* [27] and in "Myths of the Louisiana Choctaw" [28]. He compared their traditions with those of the Mississippi group as documented by Swanton and as recorded in historical sources. John H. Peterson, Jr., used Bushnell's work and Swanton's accounts, adding also a later account of Choctaw culture, to provide perspective on Choctaw history in Louisiana in the late eighteenth century [184]. Choctaw kinship terminology was studied in Oklahoma by Fred Eggan. By comparing the terms he collected with historical accounts and Swanton's work in Mississippi, he was able to show changes that he attributed to acculturation, from Mississippi to Oklahoma [77].

In 1903 the Commission to the Five Civilized Tribes, charged with carrying out the provisions of the act of 1893, sent representatives to Mississippi to encourage the Choctaws there to take allotments in Oklahoma. The activities of the Dawes Commission represent a historical continuity again in regard to the Mississippi Choctaws—that is, the attempts to persuade the remnant of the tribe living in Mississippi to take residence in Oklahoma. One can refer to John W. Wade's article "The Removal of the Mississippi Choctaws" [219] to see the pressures that were being applied, and indeed a rather large migration to Oklahoma took place in 1903. But a significant problem also arose because there appeared large numbers of individuals alleging descent from Choctaw claimants who had never been able to obtain land under Article 14 of the Treaty of Dancing Rabbit Creek. The status of these individuals was called into question, since many appeared not to be Choctaws. The problems of legitimizing these claims are treated in William Sydney Coker's article "Pat Harrison's Efforts to Reopen the Choctaw Citizenship Rolls" [47]. Of the more than 23,000 individuals alleging Choctaw citizenship, only a small percentage could prove legitimate claims, but the attraction of a major per capita distribution of funds brought forth many persons seeking admission to the final rolls of the Choctaw Nation. Harrison's attempt to open the rolls to admission of Mississippi Choctaw claimants was unsuccessful, but it did call to the attention of the United States Congress the situation of the Mississippi Choctaw communities, leading to the creation of a reservation and federal recognition of the tribe in 1918. Jesse McKee's article "The Choctaw Indians: A Geographical Study in Cultural Change" [150] discusses the situation of the Choctaws in Mississippi and the changes that Choctaw culture underwent in Oklahoma, but it is disappointingly brief in its picture of Mississippi Choctaw culture.

In contemporary American society, the Choctaws in Mississippi and Louisiana still constitute a distinctive cultural group. Hiram F. Gregory's account "Jena Band of Louisiana Choctaw" [99] concerns the struggle of the one band of the Choctaw tribe in Louisiana to achieve federal recognition. Gregory effectively demonstrates the continuity of identity between the historical communities of Mississippi and the Jena Band. John H. Peterson, Jr., has discussed the problems of "Assimilation, Separation and Out-migration in an American Indian Group" [183] in regard to the factors that have contributed to the persistence of Choctaw identity in Mississippi and to the factors that have contributed to assimilation, separation, and out-migration from the Choctaw communitites.

Although the Mississippi Choctaws have not received the attention given their Oklahoma relatives, the persistence of their cultural identity in the modern world is remarkable, and their contemporary situation is interesting in contrast to the pressure toward acculturation that the Oklahoma Choctaws have faced as a federally recognized tribe since 1830. The isolation and lack of major federal attention after 1830 may have contributed significantly to the present strong identity of the Mississippi Choctaws. Since 1969 the tribe has published *Choctaw Community News* [36], a very informative guide to current events among the Mississippi division.

The Choctaws in Mississippi did not entirely escape scholarly attention; but much of this material did not appear in published form. Three doctoral dissertations provide significant information on the history of the Choctaws in Mississippi. Eugene Ijams Farr's study of religious assimilation has the advantage of drawing on extensive records of the Baptist church and the disadvantage of concentrating almost exclusively upon Baptist influence on the Choctaws [78]. He does, however, show how strong a factor religious organization was in the cultural solidarity of the Choctaws. Charles M. Tolbert compiled significant information from commissioners' reports, census data, and other primary source material, together with fieldwork [212]. John H. Peterson, Jr., completed his dissertation in 1970 [182], and his work for and with the tribe gave him access to significant materials from the records of the tribal agency as well as an insider's perspective on the formation of the Choctaw tribal agency. His analysis of

Bureau of Indian Affairs policy toward the Mississippi Choctaws during the early years of the agency is very informative. His study clearly demonstrates that the Mississippi Choctaws have maintained their cultural heritage—politically, socially, and economically—into our own times. A dissertation that provides a perspective on Choctaw community life is that by Monte Kenaston, "Sharecropping, Solidarity and Social Cleavage: The Genesis of a Choctaw Sub-community in Tennessee" [130], in which the author records the life of a community outside Memphis, Tennessee, during the 1950s where the situation was very similar to that of the Mississippi Choctaws and whose inhabitants had significant contact with the Mississippi Choctaws.

ALPHABETICAL LIST AND INDEX

*denotes items suitable for secondary school students

American Indians: Particularly Those Adjoining to the Mississippi, East and West Florida, Georgia, South and North Carolina and Virginia. London: E. C. Dilly. Reprinted, Johnson City, Tenn.: Watauga Press, 1930; New York: Promontory Press, 1973.   (5, 16)

[5]   Aldrich, Gene. 1952. "A History of the Coal Industry in Oklahoma to 1907." Ph.D. diss., University of Oklahoma.   (53)

[6]   Allen, Virginia R. 1970. "Medical Practices and Health in the Choctaw Nation, 1831–1885." *Chronicles of Oklahoma* 48:60–73.   (37)

[7]   Andrews, Thomas F. 1965. "Freedmen in Indian Territory: A Post-Civil War Dilemma." *Journal of the West* 4:367–76.   (51)

[8]   Austin, Edward Burl. 1948. "Cyrus Byington." *Arkansas Historical Quarterly* 7:81–86.   (25)

[9]   Bailey, M. Thomas. 1972. *Reconstruction in Indian Territory: A Story of Avarice, Discrimination and Opportunism.* Port Washington, N.Y.: Kennikat Press.   (51)

[10] Baird, W. David. 1967. "Spencer Academy, Choctaw Nation, 1842–1900." *Chronicles of Oklahoma* 45:25–43.　　(43)

[11] ——. 1969. "Arkansas's Choctaw Boundary: A Study of Justice Delayed." *Arkansas Historical Quarterly* 28:201–22.　　(38)

[12] ——. 1972. *Peter Pitchlynn: Chief of the Choctaws*. Norman: University of Oklahoma Press.　　(33)

*[13] ——. 1973. *The Choctaw People*. Phoenix: Indian Tribal Series.　　(7, 57)

[14] Bartram, William. 1791. *Travels through North and South Carolina, Georgia, East and West Florida, the Cherokee Country, the Extensive Territories of the Muscogulges or Creek Confederacy, and the Country of the Choctaws. Containing an Account of the Soil and Natural Productions of Those Regions; Together with Observations on the Manners of the Indians.* Philadelphia: James and Johnson. Reprinted as *Travels of William Bartram*, ed. Mark Van Doren, New York: Dover, 1928. New ed. in facsimile, New York: Barnes and Noble, 1940. New ed., ed. Francis Harper, New Haven: Yale University Press, 1958.　　(15)

[15]   Bearss, Edwin C. 1968. "Fort Smith as the Agency for the Western Choctaws." *Arkansas Historical Quarterly* 27:40–58.   (31)

[16]   Bekkers, B. J. 1902. "The Catholic Church in Mississippi during Colonial Times." *Publications of the Mississippi Historical Society* 6:351–57.   (22)

[17]   Benson, Henry C. 1860. *Life among the Choctaw Indians and Sketches of the South-West.* Cincinnati: L. Swormstedt and A. Poe. Reprinted, New York: Johnson Reprint Corporation, 1970.   (45)

[18]   Bonnifield, Paul. 1973. "The Choctaw Nation on the Eve of the Civil War." *Journal of the West* 12:386–402.   (48)

[19]   Bossu, Jean-Bernard. 1768. *Nouveaux Voyages aux Index occidentales; Contenant une Relation des differens Peuples qui habitent les environs du grand Fleuve Saint-Louis, appellé vulgairement le Mississipi; leur Religion; leur gouvernment; leurs moeurs, leurs guerres et leur commerce.* Paris: Le Jay. 2d ed., Amsterdam: D. J. Changuion, 1769. First English ed., trans. John Reinhold Forster, published as *Travels through That Part of North*

America Formerly Called Louisiana. London: Printed for T. Davies, 1771. New ed., containing translation of 1769 ed. by Seymour Feiler, printed under title *Jean-Bernard Bossu's Travels in the Interior of North America, 1751–1762.* Norman: University of Oklahoma Press, 1962.   (6, 15)

[20] Bounds, Thelma V. 1964. *Children of Nanih Waiya.* San Antonio: Naylor Company.   (20)

[21] Bourne, Edward Gaylord, ed. 1904. *Narratives of the Career of Hernando de Soto in the Conquest of Florida, as Told by a Knight of Elvas and in the Relation by Luys Hernandez de Biedma, Factor of the Expedition, Translated by Buckingham Smith, Together with an Account of De Soto's Expedition Based on the Diary of Rodrigo Ranjel, His Private Secretary, Translated from Oviedo's Historia General y Natural de las Indias.* 2 vols. New York: Allerton Book Company. See also [190, 216].   (1)

[22] Brown, Loren N. 1931. "The Dawes Commission." *Chronicles of Oklahoma* 9:71–105.   (54)

[23] ———. 1938. "The Choctaw-Chickasaw

Court Citizens." *Chronicles of Oklahoma* 16:425–43.   (54)

[24]   ———. 1944. "The Appraisal of the Lands of the Choctaws and Chickasaws by the Dawes Commission." *Chronicles of Oklahoma* 22:177–91.   (54)

[25]   Bryce, J. Y., ed. 1928. "About Some of Our First Schools in Choctaw Nation." *Chronicles of Oklahoma* 6:354–94.   (42)

*[26]   Burt, Jesse, and Robert B. Ferguson. 1973. *Indians of the Southeast: Then and Now.* Nashville: Abingdon Press.   (8)

[27]   Bushnell, David I., Jr. 1909. *The Choctaw of Bayou Lacomb St. Tammany Parish Louisiana.* United States Bureau of American Ethnology Bulletin 48. Washington, D.C.: Government Printing Office.   (64)

[28]   ———. 1910. "Myths of the Louisiana Choctaw." *American Anthropologist,* n.s., 12:526–35.   (64)

[29]   Byington, Cyrus. 1870. "Grammar of the Choctaw Language." *Proceedings of the American Philosophical Society* 11:317–67.   (25)

[30]   ———. 1915. *A Dictionary of the Choctaw Language,* ed. John R. Swanton and H. S. Halbert. United States Bureau of American Ethnology Bulletin 46. Washington, D.C.: Government Printing Office. Reprinted, Saint Clair Shores, Mich.: Scholarly Press, 1976.   (25)

[31]   Campbell, T. N. 1951. "Medicinal Plants Used by Choctaw, Chickasaw and Creek Indians in the Early Nineteenth Century." *Journal of the Washington Academy of Sciences* 419:285–90.   (7)

[32]   ———. 1959. "The Choctaw Afterworld." *Journal of American Folklore* 72:146–54.   (7)

[33]   ———. 1959. "Choctaw Subsistence: Ethnographic Notes from the Lincecum Manuscript." *Florida Anthropologist* 12:9–24   (7)

[34]   Carter, Clarence E., comp. and ed. 1937. *The Territorial Papers of the United States.* Vol. 5. *The Territory of Mississippi 1798–1817*. Washington, D.C.: Government Printing Office.   (21)

[35]   Catlin, George. 1841. *Letters and Notes on the Manners, Customs and Condition of the North American Indians.* 2 vols. London: Toswill and Myers. Reprinted, Minneapolis: Ross and Haines, 1965; New York: Dover, 1973.   (41)

[36]   *Choctaw Community News.* 1969–   . Philadelphia, Miss.   (67)

[37]   Choctaw Nation. 1869. *Constitution and Laws of the Choctaw Nation, Together with the Treaties of 1855, 1865, 1866.* Chahta Tamaha: Published by authority of the General Council by Joseph P. Folsom. New York: W. P. Lyon and Son. Reprinted, Wilmington, Del.: Scholarly Resources, 1973.   (39)

[38]   ———. 1894. *Constitution and Laws of the Choctaw Nation, Together with the Treaties of 1837, 1855 and 1866.* Published by authority of the General Council by A. R. Durant, commissioned for the purpose, and Davis Hoover and Ben Watkins, assistant compilers. Dallas: J. F. Worley. Reprinted, Wilmington, Del.: Scholarly Resources, 1973.   (39)

[39] ———. 1897. *Acts and Resolutions of the General Council of the Choctaw Nation, Passed at Its Regular Session, Oct., 1897 and Also All the School Laws of the Choctaw Nation.* Fort Smith: n.p. Reprinted, Wilmington, Del.: Scholarly Resources, 1973. (56)

[40] ———. 1897. *Acts of Council of the Choctaw Nation, Passed at Its Regular Session of October 1895 and 1896, and the Special Session of September 1896.* Talihina, Indian Territory: Choctaw Herp. Reprinted, Wilmington, Del.: Scholarly Resources, 1973. (56)

[41] ———. 1898. *Acts and Resolutions of the General Council of the Choctaw Nation, Passed at Its Regular Session, 1898, and Its Special Session 1899.* Caddo, Indian Territory: Herald Press. Reprinted, Wilmington, Del.: Scholarly Resources, 1973. (56)

[42] ———. 1903. *Acts and Resolutions of the General Council of the Choctaw Nation, Passed at Its Regular Session 1902, and Extra Session, 1902.* Hugo, Indian Territory: Husonian Press. Reprinted, Wilmington, Del.: Scholarly Resources, 1973. (56)

[43]   ———. 1904. *Acts and Resolutions of the General Council of the Choctaw Nation, Passed at Its Regular Session, 1903.* Hugo, Indian Territory: Husonian Press. Reprinted, Wilmington, Del.: Scholarly Resources, 1973.   (56)

[44]   ———. 1978–   . *Bishinik.* Durant, Oklahoma.   (60)

[45]   Clark, Joseph Stanley. 1933. "The Eastern Boundary of Oklahoma." *Chronicles of Oklahoma* 11:1084–1110.   (38)

[46]   ———. 1955. "Immigrants in the Choctaw Coal Industry." *Chronicles of Oklahoma* 33:440–55.   (53)

[47]   Coker, William Sydney. 1964. "Pat Harrison's Efforts to Reopen the Choctaw Citizenship Rolls." *Southern Quarterly* 3:36–61.   (65)

[48]   Coleman, Michael Christopher. 1977. "Presbyterian Missionaries and Their Attitudes to the American Indians, 1837–1893." Ph.D. diss., University of Pennsylvania.   (44)

[49]   Collins, Henry B., Jr. 1927. "Potsherds

from Choctaw Village Sites in Mississippi." *Journal of the Washington Academy of Sciences* 17:259–63. (1)

[50] Copeland, C. C. 1853. "A Choctaw Tradition." *Transactions of the American Ethnological Society* 3:169–71. (7)

[51] Copeland, Charles C. 1957. "Letter Mailed from Eagle Town, Choctaw Nation, 1842." *Chronicles of Oklahoma* 35:229–33. (45)

[52] Cotterill, Robert S. 1954. *The Southern Indians: The Story of the Civilized Tribes before Removal.* Norman: University of Oklahoma Press. Reprinted, 1974. (27)

[53] Crane, Verner W. 1928. *The Southern Frontier, 1670–1732.* Durham, N.C.: Duke University Press. Reprinted, Ann Arbor: University of Michigan Press, 1956. Westport, Ct.: Greenwood Press, 1977. (9)

[54] Crockett, Bernice Norman. 1957. "Health Conditions in Indian Territory 1830 to the Civil War." *Chronicles of Oklahoma* 35:80–90. (37)

[55] ———. 1958. "Health Conditions in

the Indian Territory from the Civil War to 1890." *Chronicles of Oklahoma* 36:21–39.   (37)

[56]   Cushman, Horatio B. 1899. *History of the Choctaw, Chickasaw and Natchez Indians.* Greenville, Tex.: Headlight Printing House.   (28)

[57]   Davis, Edward. 1932. "The Mississippi Choctaw." *Chronicles of Oklahoma* 10:257–66.   (62)

[58]   Debo, Angie. 1932. "Education in the Choctaw Country after the Civil War." *Chronicles of Oklahoma* 10:383–91.   (43)

[59]   ———. 1934. *The Rise and Fall of the Choctaw Republic.* Norman: University of Oklahoma Press. 2d ed., 1961. Reprinted, 1972.   (25, 27, 36)

[60]   ———. 1940. *And Still the Waters Run: The Betrayal of the Five Civilized Tribes.* Princeton: Princeton University Press. Reprinted, 1972.   (57)

[61]   ———. 1951. *The Five Civilized Tribes of Oklahoma.* Philadelphia: Indian Rights Association.   (59)

[62] Denison, Natalie Morrison. 1946. "Missions and Missionaries of the Presbyterian Church, U.S., among the Choctaws: 1866–1907." *Chronicles of Oklahoma* 24:426–48. (44)

[63] Densmore, Frances. 1943. *Choctaw Music.* United States Bureau of American Ethnology Bulletin 136:101–88. Washington, D.C.: Government Printing Office. Reprinted, New York: Da Capo, 1972. (64)

[64] DeRosier, Arthur H., Jr. 1958. "John C. Calhoun and the Removal of the Choctaw Indians." *South Carolina Historical Association Proceedings for 1958,* pp. 33–45. (30)

[65] ———. 1959. "Pioneers with Conflicting Ideals: Christianity and Slavery in the Choctaw Nation." *Journal of Mississippi History* 21:174–89. (47)

[66] ———. 1962. "Thomas Jefferson and the Removal of the Choctaw Indians." *Southern Quarterly* 1:52–62. (30)

[67] ———. 1967. "Andrew Jackson and Negotiations for the Removal of the Choctaw Indians." *Historian* 29:343–62. (30)

[68]   ———. 1967. "The Choctaw Removal of 1831: A Civilian Effort." *Journal of the West* 6:237–47.   (30)

[69]   ———. 1970. "Negotiations for the Removal of the Choctaw: U.S. Policies of 1820 and 1830." *Chronicles of Oklahoma* 38:85–100.   (30)

[70]   ———. 1970. *The Removal of the Choctaw Indians.* Knoxville: University of Tennessee Press. Reprinted, New York: Harper and Row, 1972.   (21, 25, 29)

*[71]   ———. 1975. "The Choctaw Indians: Negotiations for Survival." In *Forked Tongues and Broken Treaties,* ed. Donald Worcester, pp. 1–31. Caldwell, Idaho: Caxton Printers.   (30)

[72]   Deupree, Mrs. N. D. 1903. "Greenwood LeFlore." *Publications of the Mississippi Historical Society* 7:141–51.   (33)

[73]   Doran, Michael F. 1975. "Population Statistics of Nineteenth Century Indian Territory." *Chronicles of Oklahoma* 53:492–515.   (37)

[74]   ———. 1976. "Antebellum Cattle

Herding in the Indian Territory." *Geographical Review* 66:48–58. (41)

[75] Edwards, John. 1932. "The Choctaw Indians in the Middle of the Nineteenth Century." *Chronicles of Oklahoma* 10:392–425. (28)

[76] ———. 1965. "An Account of My Escape from the South in 1861." *Chronicles of Oklahoma* 43:58–89. (48)

[77] Eggan, Fred. 1937. "Historical Changes in the Choctaw Kinship System." *American Anthropologist,* n.s., 39:34–52. (22, 65)

[78] Farr, Eugene Ijams. 1948. "Religious Assimilation: A Case Study of the Adoption of Christianity by the Choctaw Indians of Mississippi." Th.D. diss., New Orleans Baptist Theological Seminary. (67)

[79] Fite, Gilbert C. 1949. "Development of the Cotton Industry by the Five Civilized Tribes in Indian Territory." *Journal of Southern History* 15:342–53. (40)

[80] Foreman, Carolyn Thomas. 1928. "The Choctaw Academy." *Chronicles of Oklahoma* 6:453–80. (42)

[81]   ———. 1931. "The Choctaw Academy."
        Chronicles of Oklahoma 9:382–411.   (42)

[82]   ———. 1932. "The Choctaw Academy."
        Chronicles of Oklahoma 10:77–114.   (42)

*[83]   ———. 1936. *Oklahoma Imprints 1835–
        1907: A History of Printing in Oklahoma
        before Statehood.* Norman: University of
        Oklahoma Press.   (41)

[84]   ———. 1944. "New Hope Seminary,
        1844–1897." *Chronicles of Oklahoma*
        22:271–99.   (43)

[85]   ———. 1952. "The Armstrongs of In-
        dian Territory." *Chronicles of Oklahoma*
        30:292–307, 420–53.   (39)

*[86]   Foreman, Grant. 1930. *Indians and
        Pioneers: The Story of the American South-
        west before 1830.* New Haven: Yale Uni-
        versity Press; London: H. Milford. Rev.
        ed., Norman: University of Oklahoma
        Press, 1936. Reprinted, 1967.   (31)

*[87]   ———. 1932. *Indian Removal: The Emig-
        ration of the Five Civilized Tribes of In-
        dians.* Norman: University of Oklahoma
        Press. Reprinted, 1976   (32)

*[88]   ————. 1933. *Advancing the Frontier, 1830–1860*. Norman: University of Oklahoma Press. Reprinted, 1968.   (31)

*[89]   ————. 1934. *The Five Civilized Tribes: Cherokee, Chickasaw, Choctaw, Creek, Seminole*. Norman: University of Oklahoma Press. Reprinted, 1974.   (36)

[90]   Franks, Kenny A. 1975. "Missionaries in the West: An Expedition of the Protestant Episcopal Church in 1844." *Historical Magazine of the Protestant Episcopal Church* 44:318–33.   (45)

[91]   Gaines, George S. 1928. "Removal of the Choctaws." *Alabama State Department of Archives and History: Historical and Patriotic Series* 10:9–24.   (32)

*[92]   Gibson, Arrell M. 1971. *The Chickasaws*. Norman: University of Oklahoma Press.   (9, 39)

[93]   Gibson, Michael M. 1976. "Indian Claims in the Beds of Oklahoma Watercourses." *American Indian Law Review* 4:83–90.   (61)

[94]   Gittinger, Roy. 1917. *The Formation of*

the State of Oklahoma (1803–1906). Berkeley: University of California Press.   (54)

[95]   Goode, William Henry. 1863. *Outposts of Zion, with Limnings of Mission Life.* . . . Cincinnati: Poe and Hitchcock.   (45)

[96]   Graebner, Laura Baum. 1978. "Agriculture among the Five Civilized Tribes, 1840–1906." *Red River Valley Historical Review* 3:45–60.   (41)

[97]   Graebner, Norman Arthur. 1945. "Pioneer Indian Agriculture in Oklahoma." *Chronicles of Oklahoma* 23:232–48.   (40)

[98]   ———. 1945. "The Public Land Policy of the Five Civilized Tribes." *Chronicles of Oklahoma* 23:107–18.   (40)

[99]   Gregory, Hiram F. 1977. "Jena Band of Louisiana Choctaw." *American Indian Journal* 3(2):2–16.   (66)

[100]   Halbert, Henry S. 1882. "Courtship and Marriage among the Choctaws of Mississippi." *American Naturalist* 16:222–24.   (63)

[101]   ———. 1888. "The Choctaw Achahpih
         (Chungkee) Game." *American Antiqua-
         rian and Oriental Journal* 10:283–84.   (63)

[102]   ———. 1891. "Pyramid and Old Road
         in Mississippi." *American Antiquarian and
         Oriental Journal* 12:348–49.   (63)

[103]   ———. 1893. "Okla Hannali; or, The
         Six Towns District of the Choctaws."
         *American Antiquarian and Oriental Jour-
         nal* 15:146–49.   (63)

[104]   ———. 1894. "A Choctaw Migration
         Legend." *American Antiquarian and
         Oriental Journal* 16:215–16.   (3)

[105]   ———. 1894. "Indian Schools in
         Mississippi." *Biennial Report of the State
         Superintendent of Public Education to the
         Legislature of Mississippi for Scholastic
         Years 1891–92 and 1892–93.* Jackson,
         Miss.: Clarion Ledger Print.   (64)

[106]   ———. 1895. "The Indians in
         Mississippi and Their Schools." *Biennial
         Report of the State Superintendent of Public
         Education to the Legislature of Mississippi
         for Scholastic Years 1893–94 and 1894–
         95.* Jackson, Miss.: Clarion-Ledger
         Printing Establishment.   (64)

[107]   ———. 1898. "Indian Schools." *Biennial Report of the State Superintendent of Public Education to the Legislature of Mississippi for Scholastic Years 1895–96 and 1896–97.* Jackson, Miss.: Clarion Ledger Print.   (64)

[108]   ———. 1899. "Nanih Waiya, the Sacred Mound of the Choctaws." *Publications of the Mississippi Historical Society* 2:223–34.   (3)

[109]   ———. 1900. "Funeral Customs of the Mississippi Choctaws." *Publications of the Mississippi Historical Society* 3:353–66.   (63)

[110]   ———. 1900. "The Mississippi Choctaws." *Biennial Report of the State Superintendent of Public Instruction to the Legislature of Mississippi for Scholastic Years 1897–98 and 1898–99.* Jacksonville, Fla.: Vance Printing Company.   (64)

[111]   ———. 1901. "District Divisions of the Choctaw Nation." *Publications of the Alabama Historical Society, Miscellaneous Collections* 1:375–85.   (63)

[112]   ———. 1902. "Bernard Romans' Map of 1772." *Publications of the Mississippi Historical Society*   (16)

[113] ———. 1902. "The Last Indian Council on Noxubee River." *Publications of the Mississippi Historical Society* 4:271–80. (32)

[114] ———. 1902. "Story of the Treaty of Dancing Rabbit." *Publications of the Mississippi Historical Society* 6:373–402. (32)

[115] ———. 1903. "Origin of Mashulaville." *Publications of the Mississippi Historical Society* 7:389–97. (64)

[116] Harmon, George D. 1941. *Sixty Years of Indian Affairs.* Chapel Hill: University of North Carolina Press. Reprinted, New York: Kraus, 1969. (62)

[117] Harris, John Brice. 1959. *From Old Mobile to Fort Assumption: A Story of the French Attempts to Colonize Louisiana and Destroy the Chickasaw Indians.* Nashville: Parthenon Press. (11)

[118] Hiemstra, William L. 1948. "Early Presbyterian Missions among the Choctaw and Chickasaw Indians in Mississippi." *Journal of Mississippi History* 10:8–16. (24)

[119] ———. 1948. "Presbyterian Mis-

sionaries and Mission Churches among the Choctaw and Chickasaw Indians, 1832–1865." *Chronicles of Oklahoma* 26:459–67.   (44)

[120]   ———. 1949. "Presbyterian Mission Schools among the Choctaws and Chickasaws, 1845–1861." *Chronicles of Oklahoma* 27:33–40.   (43)

[121]   ———. 1959. "Presbyterian Missions among Choctaw and Chickasaw Indians, 1860–1861." *Presbyterian Historical Society Journal* 37:51–59.   (47)

[122]   Hodgson, Adam. 1823. *Remarks during a Journey through North America in the years 1819, 1820 and 1821, in a Series of Letters; with an Appendix, Containing an Account of Several of the Indian Tribes, and the Principal Missionary Stations, etc. Also a Letter to M. Jean Baptiste Say, on the Comparative Expense of Free and Slave Labor.* Collected, arranged and published by Samuel Whiting. New York: J. Seymour. Reprinted, Westport, Conn.: Negro Universities Press, 1970.   (24)

[123]   Holmes, Jack D. L. 1968. "The Choctaws in 1795." *Alabama Historical Quarterly* 30:33–49.   (17)

[124]   ———. 1969. "Spanish Treaties with
West Florida Indians, 1784–1802."
Florida Historical Quarterly 48:140–54.   (17)

[125]   ———. 1975. "Spanish Policy toward
the Southern Indians in the 1790s." In
Four Centuries of Southern Indians, ed.
Charles M. Hudson, pp. 65–82.
Athens: University of Georgia Press.   (17)

*[126]   Hudson, Charles. 1976. *The Southeastern
Indians.* Knoxville: University of Tennessee Press.   (8)

*[127]   Hudson, Peter James. 1939. "A Story of
Choctaw Chiefs." *Chronicles of Oklahoma*
17:7–16, 192–211.   (50)

[128]   Jeltz, Wyatt F. 1948. "The Relations of
Negroes and Choctaw and Chickasaw
Indians." *Journal of Negro History*
33:24–37. ·   (46)

[129]   Kappler, Charles J., comp. 1903–41.
Indian Affairs: Laws and Treaties. 5 vols.
Washington, D.C.: Government Print-
ing Office. Vol. 2. *Treaties,* 1904. Senate
Document no. 319, 59th Congr., 2d
sess., serial no. 4624. Reprinted, New
York: Interland, 1972.   (21)

[130] Kenaston, Monte Ray. 1972. "Share-cropping. Solidarity and Social Cleavage: The Genesis of a Choctaw Subcommunity in Tennessee." Ph.D. diss., Southern Illinois University. Ann Arbor: University Microfilms publication no. 06220.   (68)

[131] Kensell, Lewis Anthony. 1969. "Phases of Reconstruction in the Choctaw Nation, 1865–1870." *Chronicles of Oklahoma* 47:138–53.   (51)

[132] Kinnaird, Lawrence, trans, and ed. 1946–49. *Spain in the Mississippi Valley, 1765–1794.* Vols. 2–4, American Historical Association Annual Report for 1945. Three parts. Washington, D.C.: Government Printing Office.   (17)

[133] Knight, Oliver. 1953. "Fifty Years of Choctaw Law, 1834–1884." *Chronicles of Oklahoma* 31:76–95.   (39)

[134] ———. 1957. "An Oklahoma Indian Trader as a Frontiersman of Commerce." *Journal of Southern History* 23:203–19.   (53)

*[135] Lafferty, R. A. 1972. *Okla Hannali*. New
        York: Doubleday.   (35)

[136] Lanman, Charles. 1870. "Peter Pitch-
        lynn." *Atlantic Monthly* 25:486–97.   (34)

[137] LePage du Pratz, Antoine Simon. 1758.
        *Histoire de la Louisiane contenant la dé-
        couverte de ce vaste pays; sa géographique;
        un voyage dans les terres; l'histoire na-
        turelle, les moeurs, coûtumes et religion des
        naturels, avec leurs origines; deux voyages
        dans le nord du nouveau Mexique, dont un
        jusqu'à la Mer du Sud.* 3 vols. Paris: De
        Burre. 1st English ed. published as *The
        History of Louisiana, or of the Western
        Parts of Virginia and Carolina. . . ,* Lon-
        don: T. Becket and P. A. De Hondt,
        1763. Reprinted, 1774. Facsimile of
        1774 English ed., ed. Joseph G. Tregle,
        Jr., Baton Rouge: Louisiana State Uni-
        versity Press, 1975.   (15)

[138] Lewis, Anna, ed. 1939. "Diary of a
        Missionary to the Choctaws, 1860–
        1861." *Chronicles of Oklahoma* 17:428–
        47.

[139] ———, ed. 1939. "Letters regarding
        Choctaw Missions and Missionaries."
        Chronicles of Oklahoma 17:275–85.   (48)

[140]   ———. 1959. *Chief Pushmataha, American Patriot: The Story of the Choctaws' Struggle for Survival*. New York: Exposition Press.   (33)

[141]   Lewitt, Robert T. 1963. "Indian Missions and Antislavery Sentiment: A Conflict of Evangelical and Humanitarian Ideals." *Mississippi Valley Historical Review* 50:39–55.   (46)

[142]   Lincecum, Gideon. 1904. "Choctaw Traditions about Their Settlement in Mississippi and the Origin of Their Mounds." *Publications of the Mississippi Historical Society* 8:521–42.   (2)

[143]   ———. 1906. "Life of Apushimataha." *Publications of the Mississippi Historical Society* 9:415–86.   (33)

[144]   Littlefield, Daniel F., Jr., and Mary Ann Littlefield. 1976. "The Beams Family: Free Blacks in Indian Territory." *Journal of Negro History* 49:16–35.   (46)

[145]   Love, Wallace B., and R. Palmer Howard. 1970. "Health and Medical Practice in the Choctaw Nation, 1880–1907." *Journal of the Oklahoma State Medical Association* 63:124–28.   (37)

[146] Love, William A. 1903. "Mingo Moshulitubbee's Prairie Village." *Publications of the Mississippi Historical Society* 7:373–78.	(64)

[147] ———. 1910. "The Mayhew Mission to the Choctaws." *Publications of the Mississippi Historical Society* 11:363–402.	(23)

[148] McCoy, Isaac. 1840. *History of Baptist Indian Missions: Embracing Remarks on the Former and Present Condition of the Aboriginal Tribes, Their Settlement within the Indian Territory and Their Future Prospects*. Washington: William M. Morrison. Reprinted with new introduction by Robert F. Berkhofer, Jr., New York. Johnson Reprint Corporation, 1970.	(45)

[149] McCullar, Marion Ray. 1973. "The Choctaw-Chickasaw Reconstruction Treaty of 1866." *Journal of the West* 12:462–89.	(50)

[150] McKee, Jesse O. 1971. "The Choctaw Indians: A Geographical Study in Cultural Change." *Southern Quarterly* 9:107–41.	(66)

[151] McKee, Jesse O., and Jon A. Schlenker.

1980. *The Choctaws: Cultural Evolution of a Native American Tribe.* Jackson, Miss.: University Press of Mississippi.   (7, 25)

[152]   McKenzie, Douglas H. 1966. "A Summary of the Moundville Phase." *Journal of Alabama Archaeology* 12:1–58.   (1)

[153]   McLoughlin, William G. 1973. "Indian Slaveholders and Presbyterian Missionaries, 1837–1861." *Church History* 42:535–51.   (47)

[154]   ———. 1974. "The Choctaw Slave-Burning: A Crisis in Mission Work among the Indians." *Journal of the West* 13:113–27.   (47)

[155]   ———. 1974. "Red Indians, Black Slavery and White Racism: America's Slaveholding Indians." *American Quarterly* 26:367–85.   (46)

[156]   McMillan, Ethel. 1950. "First National Indian School: The Choctaw Academy." *Chronicles of Oklahoma* 28:52–62.   (42)

[157]   Marshall, Richard A. 1973. "The Prehistory of Mississippi." In *A History of*

Mississippi, ed. R. A. McLemore. Oxford: University and College Press of Mississippi. (2)

[158] Masterson, Vincent V. 1952. *The Katy Railroad and the Last Frontier*. Norman: University of Oklahoma Press. Reprinted, 1979. (52)

[159] Maxwell, Amos. 1950. "The Sequoyah Convention." *Chronicles of Oklahoma* 28:161–92, 299–340. (56)

[160] Meserve, Charles F. 1896. *The Dawes Commission and the Five Civilized Tribes of the Indian Territory*. Philadelphia: Office of the Indian Rights Association. (54)

[161] Meserve, John Bartlett. 1935. "The McCurtains." *Chronicles of Oklahoma* 13:297–312. (50)

*[162] ———. 1936. "Chief Coleman Cole." *Chronicles of Oklahoma* 14:9–21. (50)

*[163] ———. 1941. "Chief Allen Wright." *Chronicles of Oklahoma* 19:314–21. (50)

*[164] ———. 1941. "Chief Benjamin Franklin Smallwood and Chief Jeffer-

son Gardner." *Chronicles of Oklahoma* 19:213–20.   (50)

*[165]   ———. 1942. "Chief George Hudson and Chief Samuel Garland." *Chronicles of Oklahoma* 20:9–17.   (50)

[166]   Miner, H. Craig. 1976. *The Corporation and the Indian: Tribal Sovereignty and Industrial Civilization in Indian Territory, 1865–1907*. Columbia: University of Missouri Press.   (51)

[167]   Mississippi, State of. 1848. *Code of Mississippi: Being an analytical Compilation of the Public and General Statutes of the Territory and State with Tabular References to the Local and Private Acts from 1798 to 1848. With the National and State Constitutions, Assigns of the Country by the Choctaw Indians, and Acts of Congress for the Survey and Sale of the Lands and Granting Donations thereof to the State*, comp. A. Hutchison. Jackson, Miss.: Price and Fall.   (31)

[168]   Morgan, James F. 1979. "The Choctaw Warrants of 1863." *Chronicles of Oklahoma* 57:55–66.   (49)

[169] Morris, Cheryl Haun. 1972. "Choctaw and Chickasaw Indian Agents, 1831–1874." *Chronicles of Oklahoma* 50:415–36. (39)

[170] Morrison, James D. 1949. "News for the Choctaws." *Chronicles of Oklahoma* 27:207–22. (41)

[171] ———. 1951. "Social History of the Choctaw, 1865–1907." Ph.D. diss., University of Oklahoma. (49)

[172] ———. 1954. "Problems in the Industrial Progress and Development of the Choctaw Nation, 1865–1907." *Chronicles of Oklahoma* 32:71–91. (50)

[173] ———. 1960. "Note on Abolitionism in the Choctaw Nation." *Chronicles of Oklahoma* 38:78–83. (47)

[174] Morrison, William B. 1926. "The Choctaw Mission of the American Board of Commissioners for Foreign Missions." *Chronicles of Oklahoma* 4:166–83. (45)

[175] ———. 1932. *The Red Man's Trail.* Richmond, Va.: Presbyterian Committee of Publication. (44)

[176] Nash, Charles H. 1972. *Chucalissa: Excavations and Burials through 1963.* Occasional Papers no. 6. Memphis: Memphis State University Anthropological Research Center. (2)

[177] *The New American State Papers: Indian Affairs.* 1972. 13 vols. Wilmington, Del.: Scholarly Resources. (18)

[178] O'Donnell, James H., III. 1973. *Southern Indians in the American Revolution.* Knoxville: University of Tennessee Press. (12)

[179] Paape, Charles W. 1946. "The Choctaw Revolt: A Chapter in the Intercolonial Rivalry in the Old Southwest." Ph.D. diss., University of Illinois, Urbana. (12)

[180] Peebles, Christopher S. 1979. "Moundville: The Social Organization of a Prehistoric Community and Culture." Ph.D. diss., University of California, Santa Barbara. (1)

[181] Penman, John T. 1978. "Historic Choctaw Towns of the Southern Division." *Journal of Mississippi History* 40:132–41. (2)

[182] Peterson, John H., Jr. 1970. "The Mississippi Band of Choctaw Indians: Their Recent History and Current Social Relations." Ph.D. diss., University of Georgia. Ann Arbor: University Microfilm Publication no. 13106. (67)

[183] ——. 1972. "Assimilation, Separation and Out-migration in an American Indian Group." *American Anthropologist*, n.s., 74:1286–89. (66)

[184] ——. 1975. "Louisiana Choctaw Life at the End of the Eighteenth Century." In *Four Centuries of Southern Indians*, ed. Charles M. Hudson, pp. 101–13. Athens: University of Georgia Press. (64)

[185] Phelps, Dawson A. 1952. "The Choctaw Mission: An Experiment in Civilization." *Journal of Mississippi History* 14:35–62. (24)

[186] Plaisance, Aloysius. 1954. "The Choctaw Trading House, 1803–1822." *Alabama Historical Quarterly* 16:393–423. (18)

[187] Quinten, B. T. 1967. "Oklahoma Tribes, the Great Depression and the Indian Bureau." *Mid-America: An Historical Review* 49:29–43. (58)

[188]   Rampp, Lary C., and Donald A.
         Rampp. 1975. *The Civil War in the In-
         dian Territory*. Austin, Tex.: Presidial
         Press.   (49)

[189]   Riley, Franklin L. 1904. "Choctaw Land
         Claims." *Publications of the Mississippi
         Historical Society* 8:345–95.   (62)

[190]   Robertson, James Alexander, trans.
         and ed. 1932–33. *True Relation of the
         Hardships Suffered by Govenor Fernando
         de Soto and Certain Portuguese Gentlemen
         during the Discovery of the Province of
         Florida. Now Newly Set Forth by a Gentle-
         man of Elvas*. Vol. 1: Facsimile repro-
         duction of 1557 Portuguese edition
         entitled *Relacam Verdadeira*. . . . Vol. 2.
         English translation with notes. De
         Land: Florida Historical Society.   (1)

[191]   Romans, Bernard. 1775. *A Concise Nat-
         ural History of East and West Florida: Con-
         taining an Account of the Natural Produce
         of all the Southern Part of British America*
         . . . New York: Printed for the author.
         Reprinted, Gretna, La.: Pelican, 1961.   (16)

[192]   Rouse, Mrs. Shelley D. 1916. "Colonel
         Dick Johnson's Choctaw Academy: A

Forgotten Educational Experiment."
Ohio Archaeological and Historical Publications 25:88–117. (42)

[193] Rowland, Dunbar, ed. 1905. *The Mississippi Territorial Archives, 1798–1803.* Nashville, Tenn.: Press of Brandon Printing Company. (21)

[194] ———. 1911. *Mississippi Provincial Archives, 1763–66: English Dominion.* Nashville, Tenn.: Press of Brandon Printing Company. (12)

[195] Rowland, Dunbar, and A. G. Sanders, eds. 1927–32. *Mississippi Provincial Archives: French Dominion.* 3 vols. Jackson: Press of the Mississippi Department of Archives and History. (9)

[196] Royce, Charles C., comp. *Indian Land Cessions in the United States.* In *Eighteenth Annual Report of the Bureau of American Ethnology,* pp. 521–997. Washington, D.C.: Government Printing Office. Reprinted, N.Y.: Arno, 1971; N.Y.: AMS, 1973. (21)

[197] Satz, Ronald N. 1975. *American Indian Policy in the Jacksonian Era.* Lincoln: University of Nebraska Press. (31)

[198]   Schoolcraft, Henry Rowe. 1860. *Archives of Aboriginal Knowledge: Containing All the Original Papers Laid Before Congress Respecting the History, Antiquities, Language, Ethnology, Pictography, Rites, Superstitions, and Mythology, of the Indian Tribes of the United States.* 6 vols. Philadelphia, J. B. Lippincott. Reprint of first 5 vols. with index and slight changes in text of *Historical and Statistical Information Respecting the History, Condition and Prospects of the Indian Tribes of the United States . . . ,* illustrated by Seth Eastman. Philadelphia: Lippincott, Brambo, 1851–57.   (41)

[199]   Serrano y Sanz, Manuel. 1916. *España y los Indios Cherokis y Chactas en la Segunda Mitad del Siglo XVIII.* Seville: Tip. de la "Guia Oficial."   (17)

[200]   Smith, Allene DeShazo. 1951. *Greenwood LeFlore and the Choctaw Indians of the Mississippi Valley.* Memphis: C. A. Davis Printing Company.   (33)

[201]   Smith, Calvin C. 1975. "The Oppressed Oppressors: Negro Slavery among the Choctaw Indians of Oklahoma." *Red River Valley Historical Review* 2:240–53.   (46)

[202] Spalding, Arminta Scott. 1967. "From the Natchez Trace to Oklahoma: Development of Christian Civilization among the Choctaws, 1800–1860." *Chronicles of Oklahoma* 45:2–24. (24)

[203] ———. 1975. "Cyrus Kingsbury: Missionary to the Choctaws." Ph.D. diss., University of Oklahoma. Ann Arbor: University Microfilms publication no. 21197. (25)

[204] Spear, Eloise G. 1977. "Choctaw Indian Education with Special Reference to Choctaw County, Oklahoma: An Historical Approach." Ph.D. diss., University of Oklahoma. Ann Arbor: University Microfilms publication no. 32883. (42)

[205] Swanton, John R. 1911. *Indian Tribes of the Lower Mississippi Valley and Adjacent Coast of the Gulf of Mexico.* Bureau of American Ethnology Bulletin 43. Washington, D.C.: Government Printing Office. (7, 27)

[206] ———. 1918. "An Early Account of the Choctaw Indians." *Memoirs of the American Anthropological Association* 5:53–72. (13, 14)

[207]   ———. 1929. *Myths and Tales of the Southeastern Indians*. United States Bureau of American Ethnology Bulletin 88. Washington, D.C.: Government Printing Office. Reprinted, New York: AMS, 1976.   (7, 27)

[208]   ———. 1931. *Source Material for the Social and Ceremonial Life of the Choctaw Indians*. United States Bureau of American Ethnology Bulletin 103. Washington, D.C.: Government Printing Office. (3, 27)

[209]   ———. 1946. *The Indians of the Southeastern United States*. Bureau of American Ethnology Bulletin 137. Washington, D.C.: Government Printing Office. (7, 27)

[210]   Syndergaard, Rex. 1974. "The Final Move of the Choctaws." *Chronicles of Oklahoma* 52:207–19.   (31)

[211]   Taylor, Lyda A. 1940. *Plants Used as Curatives by Certain Southeastern Tribes*. Cambridge, Mass.: Botanical Museum of Harvard University.   (7)

[212]   Tolbert, Charles M. 1958. "A Sociological Study of the Choctaw Indians in Mississippi." Ph.D. diss., Louisiana State

University. Ann Arbor: University Microfilms publication no. 02856. (67)

[213] United States Census Office. 11th Census (1890). 1894. *Extra Census Bulletin: The Five Civilized Tribes in Indian Territory; The Cherokees, Chickasaw, Choctaw, Creek and Seminole Nations.* Washington, D.C.: United States Census Printing Office. (54)

[214] United States Subsistence Department. 1834–35. *Indian Removals: Correspondence on the Subject of the Emigration of Indians, between 30th November 1831 and 27th December 1833.* 5 vols. Washington, D.C.: Government Printing Office. Reprinted, New York· AMS, 1974. (32)

[215] United States War Department. 1789–1848. *Annual Reports of the Commissioner of Indian Affairs.* Washington, D.C.: Government Printing Office. (21)

[216] Varner, John Grier, and Jeanette Johnson Varner, trans, 1951. *The Florida of the Inca: A History of the Adelantado Hernando de Soto, Governor and Captain General of the Kingdom of Florida, and*

of Other Heroic Spanish and Indian Cavaliers, Written by the Inca, Garcilasco de la Vega. Austin: University of Texas Press. Originally published as *La Florida del Ynca*. Lisbon: Pedro Crasbeeck, 1605. Many editions available in translation.   (1)

[217]   Villiers du Terrage, M. de. 1922. "Documents concernant l'histoire des Indians de la région orientale de la Louisiane." *Journal de la Société des Américainistes*, n. s., 14:127–40.   (10)

[218]   ———. 1923. "Notes sur les Chactas." *Journal de la Société des Américainistes*, n.s., 15:223–50.   (10)

[219]   Wade, John William. 1904. "The Removal of the Mississippi Choctaws." *Publications of the Mississippi Historical Society* 8:397–426.   (65)

*[220]   Walthall, John A. 1977. *Moundville: An Introduction to the Archaeology of a Mississippian Chiefdom*. Tuscaloosa: Alabama Museum of Natural History.   (1)

[221]   Watkins, John A. 1894. "The Choctaws in Mississippi." *American Antiquarian and Oriental Journal* 16:69–77.   (29)

[222]   ———. 1894. "A Contribution to Chacta History." *American Antiquarian and Oriental Journal* 16:257–65.   (29)

[223]   Willis, William S. 1957. "The Nation of Bread." *Ethnohistory* 4:125–49.   (16)

[224]   Wilson, T. Paul. 1975. "Delegates of the Five Civilized Tribes to the Confederate Congress." *Chronicles of Oklahoma* 53:353–66.   (40)

[225]   Woods, Patricia Dillon. 1978. "The Relations between the French of Colonial Louisiana and the Choctaw, Chickasaw and Natchez Indians, 1699–1762." Ph.D. diss., Louisiana State University. Ann Arbor: University Microfilms publication no. 11595.   (11)

[226]   Wright, Alfred. 1828. "Choctaws." *Missionary Herald* 25:187–88.   (24)

[227]   Wright, Muriel H. 1928. "The Removal of the Choctaws to the Indian Territory, 1830–1833." *Chronicles of Oklahoma* 6:103–28.   (32)

[228]   ———. 1929. "Brief Outline of the Choctaw and the Chickasaw Nations in

the Indian Territory, 1820 to 1860."
Chronicles of Oklahoma 7:388–415.   (36)

[229]   ———. 1930. "Organization of Counties in the Choctaw and Chickasaw Nations." *Chronicles of Oklahoma* 8:315–34.   (39)

[230]   ———. 1932. "A Brief Review of the
Life of Doctor Eliphalet Nott Wright."
Chronicles of Oklahoma 10:267–86.   (57)

*[231]   ———. 1951. *A Guide to the Indian Tribes
of Oklahoma*. Norman: University of Oklahoma Press. Reprinted, 1977.   (36, 57)

[232]   ———. 1954. "General Douglas H.
Cooper, C.S.A." *Chronicles of Oklahoma*
32:142–84.   (49)

[233]   Wright, Muriel H., and George M.
Shirk. 1953. "Artist Möllhausen in
Oklahoma—1853." *Chronicles of Okla-
homa* 31:392–441.   (41)

[234]   Young, Mary Elizabeth. 1961. *Redskins,
Ruffleshirts and Rednecks: Indian
Allotments in Alabama and Mississippi,
1830–1860*. Norman: University of Ok-
lahoma Press.   (62)

The Newberry Library
Center for the History of the American Indian
Founding Director: D'Arcy McNickle
Director: Francis Jennings

Established in 1972 by the Newberry Library, in conjunction with the Committee on Institutional Cooperation of eleven midwestern universities, the Center makes the resources of one of America's foremost research libraries in the Humanities available to those interested in improving the quality and effectiveness of teaching American Indian history. The Newberry's collections include some 100,000 volumes on the history of the American Indian and offer specialized resources for studying historical aspects of Indian-White relations and Indian linguistics. The Center also assists Native Americans engaged in writing tribal histories and developing educational materials.

ADVISORY COMMITTE